IMAGES
of America

ROUTE 66 IN
ARIZONA

On March 27, 1928, the runners in the Bunion Derby transcontinental footrace passed the general store at Flagstaff. Eventual winner Andy Payne is shown here. That day, Payne lagged 30 minutes behind leader Nestor Erickson. The runners struggled up 49 Hill, the highest altitude on the route at 7,410 feet. They had run 500 grueling miles in two weeks. (Cline Library.)

ON THE COVER: The 1972 Eagles hit "Take it Easy" put Winslow on the map. Jackson Browne and Glenn Frey wrote the song with the line, "Standin' on a corner in Winslow, Arizona." Decades before the song, this man was standing on the corner at Second Street and Kinsley Street, now Standin' on the Corner Park. A mural and a statue of a musician in the park illustrate the song. (Joe Sonderman.)

IMAGES
of America

ROUTE 66 IN ARIZONA

Joe Sonderman

ARCADIA
PUBLISHING

Published by Arcadia Publishing
Charleston, South Carolina

Library of Congress Control Number: 2010926985

For all general information, please contact Arcadia Publishing:
Telephone 843-853-2070
Fax 843-853-0044
E-mail sales@arcadiapublishing.com
For customer service and orders:
Toll-Free 1-888-313-2665

Visit us on the Internet at www.arcadiapublishing.com

For Lorraine, Cathy, and Kim

CONTENTS

ACKNOWLEDGMENTS

A book on Route 66 would be impossible without the inspiration of Michael Wallis and works by Thomas Arthur Repp, David Wickline, Quinta Scott, and Marshall Trimble. Jim Hinckley and Michael Ward provided invaluable assistance and images, along with Steve Rider and Phillip Gordon. Thank you to Jared Jackson and Mike Litchfield at Arcadia Publishing. Unless otherwise noted, images are from the author's collection.

INTRODUCTION

From the start, this was no ordinary road, because it was blazed by camels. In 1857, Lt. Edward F. Beale surveyed a wagon road from Fort Defiance, New Mexico, to the Colorado River along the 35th Parallel. The expedition brought along 23 camels to test their usefulness in hauling cargo. The camels were turned loose, and their descendants were spotted into the 20th century.

The Atlantic and Pacific Railroad (later the Santa Fe) closely followed Beale's wagon road, spawning the communities of Holbrook, Winslow, Flagstaff, Williams, Ashfork, Seligman, Kingman, and others. The Fred Harvey Company opened Arizona to mass tourism, constructing lavish Harvey Houses that offered Santa Fe Railroad patrons and locals food and accommodations equal to those in the major cities. The Harvey Houses were ready to serve motorists when the automobile age arrived.

In 1909, J. B. Girand was appointed as territorial engineer to lay out four roads connecting each of the 14 Arizona county seats. One of those roads passed through Springerville and St. Johns before picking up the future path of Route 66. Girand's route also dropped south from Kingman through Yucca and Topock to the Colorado River.

By this time, private promoters were laying out routes with fancy names across the nation. Many spent little on maintenance and took travelers miles out of their way past businesses that made contributions. A bewildering array of non-standardized symbols and color codes marked the trails, which often overlapped.

In 1913, an association mapped out the National Old Trails Road through Arizona, following Girand's route with two exceptions. The new route followed the railroad west from Gallup, New Mexico, via Lupton to Holbrook. At Kingman, the Old Trails Highway headed west across the Black Mountains to Oatman, a very important town at the time. Girand's route between Springerville and Holbrook became a branch of the Old Trails Road.

In 1925, the federal government stepped in to ease the confusion, and a committee assigned numbers to the proposed national routes. East-west routes were given even numbers, with the most important routes ending in "0." The north-south routes received odd numbers, with a number ending in "5" denoting the major highways. Cyrus Avery of Tulsa, Oklahoma, led the committee. He made sure the important-sounding "60" was assigned to the highway between Chicago and Los Angeles through his hometown, even though it was not a true east-west transcontinental route.

Kentucky officials were outraged. Gov. William J. Fields wanted 60 for the transcontinental route through his state. After a battle of angry telegrams, it was agreed that the catchy sounding "66" was acceptable for the Los Angeles–to–Chicago highway. Route 66 would follow the National Old Trails Road through Arizona.

The national highway system went into effect on November 11, 1926, and the newly formed Route 66 Association went to work promoting the highway. Association publicity man Lon Scott came up with the idea of a transcontinental footrace. Nearly 300 runners in the Bunion Derby, promoted by the flamboyant C. C. Pyle, left Los Angeles on March 4, 1928, and the media avidly followed. On March 12, the 127 remaining runners were ferried into Arizona, and they crossed into New Mexico on March 22. Just 55 runners made it to New York City. Andy Payne, a half Cherokee from the Route 66 community of Foyil, Oklahoma, took the $25,000 first prize. Pyle lost thousands of dollars because he expected communities to pay for the privilege of hosting the runners and the accompany bizarre sideshow, but several refused. Route 66 reaped the publicity.

During the Great Depression, thousands of Dust Bowl refugees fled west. In *The Grapes of Wrath*, John Steinbeck called 66 "The Mother Road, the road of flight." For many of those living along the highway in Arizona, Route 66 provided an economic lifeline. The last segment of Route 66 to be paved in Arizona was at Crozier Canyon, a 3.9-mile project completed on July 13, 1937. Route 66 was paved from coast to coast by mid-1938.

During World War II, Route 66 was vital for moving troops and equipment to installations such as the Navajo Army Depot at Bellemont. Another great migration took place as people sought defense jobs in California. Rationing of tires and gasoline curtailed recreational traveling. The glory years of Route 66 began when the war ended.

In 1946, Bobby Troup's "Route 66" became a huge hit for Nat King Cole, further romanticizing Route 66. Americans hit the road in record numbers, and all manner of motels, cafés, gas stations, roadside zoos, and trading posts sprang up. Beginning in 1960, the CBS television series *Route 66* added to the allure.

By that time, the popularity of Route 66 was proving to be its downfall. The torturous route through Oatman was bypassed in 1952. The new route returned to Girand's pathway south from Kingman through Yucca and Topock. In 1956, one out of every six traffic deaths in Arizona occurred on "Bloody 66." In 1959, in just one month, 11 people died on a stretch of Route 66 near Peach Springs.

Congress passed the Interstate Highway Act in 1956, authorizing a 41,000-mile system of divided superhighways that would go around the towns where Route 66 was "The Main Street of America."

Interstate 40 was completed around Flagstaff in 1968, between Ashfork and Kingman in 1975, around Winslow in 1979, and past Holbrook in 1981. A bittersweet ceremony on October 13, 1984, marked the opening of Interstate 40 around Williams, the last community on Route 66 to be bypassed. In 1985, Route 66 was officially decertified. But "The Mother Road" didn't die.

Angel Delgadillo, a barber in Seligman, gathered a group of business owners who formed the Route 66 Association of Arizona in February 1987. With Angel as an unofficial spokesman dubbed the "Guardian Angel of Route 66," their efforts sparked a revival that spread along the entire highway. In November 1987, the Arizona Legislature designated Route 66 between Seligman and Kingman as "Historic Route 66," a designation later applied to the entire route in Arizona. Today travelers come from all over the world to experience a time when getting there was half the fun. Adventure waits at the Interstate 40 off-ramp.

One

NEW MEXICO LINE TO THE PETRIFIED FOREST

Motorists crossing the state line from New Mexico into Arizona saw this billboard, touting some of the natural wonders ahead, erected by the Arizona unit of the U.S. Highway 66 Association. Trading posts and curio stores line the highway at Lupton, named for the man who established the first trading post here.

The state line runs right through the Fort Chief Yellowhorse Trading Post, with its fake animals perched on the bluff. Chief Juan Yellowhorse bought Harry "Indian" Miller's trading post at the Cave of the Seven Devils in 1960, and the post is still operated by the chief's family. Billboards for the post said, "We No Scalpum Paleface. Just Scalpum Wallet."

The Ortega family began trading with American Indians in the mid-1800s. Max and Amelia Ortega opened the Indian Trails Trading Post at Lupton on June 21, 1946. Their son, Armand Ortega, is now one of the world's foremost American Indian jewelry dealers. The trading post was demolished to make room for the Interstate 40 service road in 1965.

Claude and Clara Lee owned the Querino Canyon Trading Post and bought Big Arrows from Slim Brazier. When Route 66 was relocated in the 1950s, they abandoned Querino Canyon and built a new Big Arrows. Their daughter Arlene and her husband, Jay Crone, managed it into the late 1960s, offering Arlene's "Squaw Dress Originals."

Corporal Agarn, Sergeant O'Rourke, and the Hekawi Indians never were actually here, but the Fort Courage Trading Post at Houck was based on the 1960s television series *F Troop*. This good old-fashioned tourist trap was originally constructed by the Van de Camps. Later owned by Bill Gipe, J. T. Turner, and Armand Ortega, Fort Courage is now a modern trading post just off the interstate.

Al Berry operated the Log Cabin Trading Post near Sanders, built of pine logs and known for illicit gambling. Berry advertised the "Largest Free Zoo in the Southwest" and charged tourists to see American Indian ruins he had excavated. Only some ruins and a forlorn wishing well remain today west of the Indian Ruins Store operated by Armand Ortega.

The White Elephant bar, lodge and curio store was originally the Chamese Lodge, constructed by Mitchell Dickens and Robert Cassady Jr. There reportedly were illegal slot machines inside. Al Berry bought the lodge after it went bankrupt and later traded the property to Skeet and Maude Eddens. The White Elephant was destroyed by fire.

The Navapache Café was located in Chambers, named for trading post operator Charles Chambers. Other businesses here included the Cedar Point Trading Post and the original Chambers Trading Post, later owned by Alice and Frank Young. They built the Chieftain Motel on Interstate 40 when Chambers was bypassed.

Charley Jacobs built a very successful business because he was one of the few craftsmen who could cut brittle petrified wood for jewelry. To attract even more business, Jacobs invited Navajo families to sell their rugs, jewelry, and other items while living year-round at his "Navajo Village" west of Chambers. His wandering burros also lured tourists.

Harry C. Osborne operated the Painted Desert Point Trading Post, 21 miles east of Holbrook. There were illegal slot machines inside, the take split with the operators of the Chamese Lodge farther east on Route 66. In 1952, the 78-year-old Osborne shot and killed his mentally ill son, Lee, at the trading post. A coroner's jury ruled he acted in self defense. (Phil Gordon.)

Dotch and Alberta Windsor opened the Painted Desert Trading Post in 1942. They divorced in 1950, and Dotch married Joy Nevin. They advertised a 150-pound canary. When disappointed tourists found it was just a burro, Dotch informed them that prospectors called the burro "the canary of the desert." The post was abandoned after Dotch and Joy split up in 1956, and the lonely ruins remain. (Steve Rider.)

Julia Grant Miller was the sister of Harry "Indian" Miller, owner of the infamous Fort Two Guns at Canyon Diablo. Her Painted Desert Park offered a spectacular view of the Painted Desert. Julia battled with Charles "White Mountain" Smith, superintendent of the Petrified Forest, who said her establishment was unsanitary and unsightly. A lion at the zoo once scalped a visitor.

Julia's son, Charley Jacobs, returned to his mother's land in 1953 and constructed a new trading post and tower. It was partly an effort to get the National Park Service to buy the land before Route 66 was relocated. Since the property was within the Petrified Forest National Monument, the NPS was upset by the "eyesore" and bought Charley's land in 1958. The post was destroyed. (National Park Service.)

The Painted Desert is a marvel of strange landscapes. Bands of colored sediments and clay of the Chinle rock formation have been exposed by erosion, and the beautiful palette changes as the sun moves across the sky. In September 1932, Pres. Herbert Hoover made 53,300 acres part of the Petrified Forest National Monument, now Petrified Forest National Park.

The Painted Desert Inn was originally the Stone Tree House, constructed with petrified wood by Herbert D. Lore in 1924 and purchased by the government in 1936. The Civilian Conservation Corps remodeled it into a Pueblo Revival–style structure. The Fred Harvey Company ran the hotel from 1947 until April 16, 1963. Nearly demolished in 1975, it is now a museum and visitors center.

16

Two

PETRIFIED FOREST TO HOLBROOK

Over 200 million years ago, this area was a vast floodplain where stately pine trees grew. Sand and volcanic ash covered the fallen trees, and over the eons, silica replaced the wood. After the area was lifted above sea level, wind and water eroded the sandstone and shale surrounding the petrified logs, leaving them on the surface today.

After the completion of the Santa Fe Railroad, vast amounts of petrified wood were looted to be sold to tourists. That came to an end after December 8, 1906, when Pres. Theodore Roosevelt declared the Petrified Forest a national monument. It became a national park in 1962, the only national park to include a section of Route 66. A member of the Nez Perce tribe is shown here next to a log dubbed "Old Faithful."

Route 66 could be a dangerous highway. On August 24, 1944, the driver of this Red Bluff oil truck and two soldiers burned to death when the truck overturned and exploded east of Holbrook. The soldiers' vehicle had stalled on the other side of the highway when the truck driver pulled out to pass. (Michael Luke.)

Holbrook was the headquarters for the Whiting Brothers chain of gas stations, which once had over 100 locations in the southwest. The company also operated about 15 motels, including two in Holbrook. The Whiting Brothers Motel at 2402 Navajo Boulevard became the Sahara Inn and has a distinctive saw tooth gabled roof.

The 26-unit 66 Motel at 2105 Navajo Boulevard opened in 1948. R. R. Rogers was the owner. It was later owned by Mr. and Mrs. H. S. Harvey. The café became Bob Lyall's 66 Steak House in the 1950s. It then became the Hilltop Café, operated by Ray and Barbara Williams. The 66 Motel and Hilltop Café are still in business today.

At Young's Corral, they said, "A stranger is a friend we haven't met—yet!" Located at 865 Navajo Boulevard, Young's opened in 1948 and is still a popular watering hole today. Murals on the side of the building show a historical view and celebrate the Corral's Route 66 heritage. The unusual sign out front features the tail end of a horse.

Jack Paine originally owned the Pow Wow Trading Post, later purchased by Edward and Pauline Leopold. Their son Ken and his wife, Gwen, took over in 1946. A massive Kachina sign (upper left) now stands in front of the Pow Wow. The wording was changed from "Motel" to "Rocks" when the motel units were converted into the rock shop.

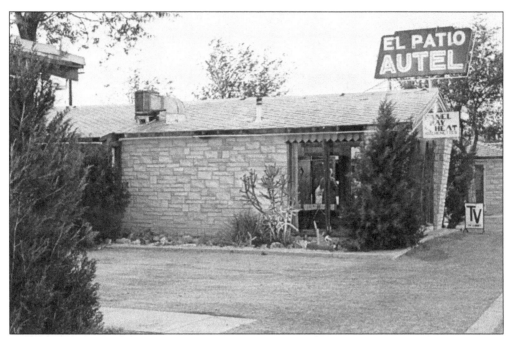

Ken and Gwen Leopold also owned the El Patio Autel across the street from the Pow Wow. Later the El Patio Motel, it was once the home of an intimidating-looking chair made from five and a half sets of elk horns. Gwen's grandfather Edward Leopold made the chair, later moved to the Holbrook Elks Lodge. The motel no longer stands.

The Holbrook Motel at 720 Navajo Boulevard advertised as a new motel in 1958. There were 62 modern units promoted as being away from the railroad noise. The motel boasted "Wall-to-wall carpeting, refrigerated air-conditioning, and individually controlled wall heaters." It became the America's Best Value Inn.

Built in 1898, the old Navajo County Courthouse is now a museum reportedly haunted by the ghost of George Smiley. Smiley was slated to hang for murder on December 8, 1899. But the press got hold of a cheerfully worded invitation to the necktie party issued by Sheriff Frank Wattron. Arizona governor Nathan Oakes Murphy reprimanded Wattron and issued a 30-day stay. Smiley did hang on January 8, 1900, after more subdued invitations were issued.

Looking south on Navajo Boulevard approaching Arizona Street in Holbrook, the Green Lantern Café is at right. Originally located further south, it was operated for many years by Nevert and Gilbert Scorse and was recommended by Jack Ritttenhouse in his *Guidebook to Route 66*. This building was occupied by a music store and a shoe store as of 2010.

Holbrook is named for Henry Holbrook, chief engineer for the Atlantic and Pacific Railroad. The view looks north on Navajo Boulevard at West Hopi Drive. Chester B. Campbell's Coffee House opened in 1928 and was known for Son-of-a-Bitch Stew, a cowboy dish made with the heart, liver, brains, and other calf organs.

Dick Mester operated Campbell's Coffee House during World War II and then opened his own place catering to bus passengers on that site. Mester's Automat Cafeteria advertised as the "First eating establishment of this kind in Arizona." The building at the southeast corner of Navajo Boulevard and Hopi Drive still stands.

The Holbrook area is a haven for roadside dinosaurs. These were made by Adam Luna, owner of the Rainbow Rock Shop at 101 Navajo Boulevard. There is a bronze dinosaur sculpture in the city park just a block away, and comical dinosaurs chomp on bloody mannequins at Stewart's Petrified Wood, east of town on Interstate 40.

Joe and Aggie Montano opened their café in 1943. In 1965, they moved to the location shown here at 120 West Hopi Drive. The building had formerly housed the Cactus Café. Their daughter Alice and her husband, Stanley Gallegos, took over in 1978. Today, their children run Joe and Aggie's Café, the oldest restaurant in Holbrook.

The 26-unit Woods Inn at 235 West Hopi Drive opened in 1960 and was later known as Pope's Inn. It is still in operation today as the Holbrook Inn. Motels such as this one thrived much longer than in many Route 66 communities, because Holbrook was not bypassed until 1981. After the interstate opened, 45 businesses closed within a year.

CHIEF
JOE SEKAKUKU
A Hopi
Snake Chief

Chief Joe's Trading Post, which stood at 510 West Hopi Drive, was one of the few actually owned by an American Indian. Joe Sekakuku once worked for the Fred Harvey Company, performing Hopi snake dances for tourists at the Grand Canyon. His original post was at Two Guns, and he was a witness at the murder trail of Harry Miller (see page 52).

Built, owned, and operated by Ed and Mae Burton, the ranch-style Western Motel at 521 West Hopi Drive originally had 21 units, later expanded to 26. The old sign featuring a smiling cowboy was moved to the Butterfield Stage Company Steakhouse next door, and the motel is now a storage business.

The Chief Motel, at 608 West Hopi Drive, was originally the Exclusive Motel. Owned by William Finder, it burned suspiciously in 1975. Finder's Commercial Hotel in Flagstaff was also torched hours after being condemned that same year. A parking lot wall on the Chief site features a big painted map of Route 66 advertising the Butterfield Stage Company Steakhouse across the street.

The Motoraunt Coffee Shop, Dining Room, and "Refined Cocktail Bar" opened on March 27, 1947. It offered arts and crafts by Navajo Indians, and organist Fred Laskowsky was regularly on hand to play requests. The Motoraunt developed into the Butterfield Stage Company Steakhouse in the 1970s, complete with a stagecoach perched on the roof.

The Sea Shell Motel at 612 West Hopi Drive was part of a small chain. There were also Sea Shell Motels in Lordsburg, New Mexico; Blythe, California; Safford, Arizona; and Gila Bend, Arizona. The expanded Sea Shell later became a Whiting Brothers Motor Hotel, then the Golden Door Motor Hotel, and finally the Economy Inn.

In 1938, Chester Lewis saw Frank Redford's Wigwam Village No. 2 at Cave City, Kentucky, and decided to build one of his own. Wigwam Village No. 6 opened on June 1, 1950. Redford was paid the proceeds from pay radios in the rooms in return for use of the plans. Texaco later ordered Lewis to replace the large wigwam in the center with a traditional station.

The Wigwam closed in 1974 and was vacant until 1988. Its future was in doubt after Chester Lewis died in 1986. But the Lewis family restored the 15 steel-framed and stucco-covered wigwams. In this 1954 view, the Forest Motel is visible across Route 66. It was owned by Kale and Beulah Soehner, and a supermarket now occupies the site.

The Sundown Dining Room and Coffee Shop was adjacent to the Sundown Motel, owned by Albert and Jack Ong. Fern Daugherty was also an operator of the 26-unit motel one block west of the Wigwam. The motel and the former restaurant building are still standing as of 2010 along with the big sign, which has been covered with white paint.

In 1956, the Whiting Brothers DeLuxe Motel at 902 West Hopi Drive was expanded to become the Whiting Motor Hotel with the Kolob Restaurant next door. Al and Helene Frycek advertised it as "A new motel designed and furnished for your comfort." There were 57 units with "individually controlled hi-fi music."

The Whiting Motor Hotel became the Sun N' Sand Motel, still operated by Al and Helene Frycek at the time of this view. It closed in 2001. According to the city of Holbrook, owner Robert McIntosh neglected the property. As of 2010, the Sun N' Sand is still standing but is boarded up. The shell of the sign remains.

The Plainsman Restaurant at 1001 West Hopi Drive recalls the days when cowboys of the Aztec Land and Cattle Company, or the "Hashknife Outfit," terrorized Holbrook. There were 26 shooting deaths in 1886, when the population was about 250. The restaurant closed in 2005 but was later renovated by Jon and Carol States.

The Desert View Lodge at 1009 West Hopi Drive was owned and operated by Ruby and Jim McDermott and originally had 23 units. It was later owned by Norm and Adelyne Hormandl. In 1956, an 11-unit second deck was added, and the Desert View Lodge became the first motel in Holbrook with a swimming pool. It became the Star Inn.

These motorists are lined up at the Arizona Department of Agriculture and Horticulture Inspection Station just west of Holbrook. R. P. Harvey served as the chief inspector. In 1946, about 35,000 westbound vehicles passed through the station each month. By July 1959, that number had risen to 100,869.

Three

JOSEPH CITY TO WINSLOW

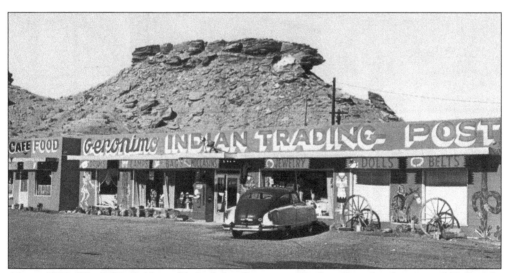

About 1950, "Doc" Hatfield established the Geronimo Trading Post 5 miles west of Holbrook. Carl Kempton took over in 1967. In 1974, he constructed the current Geronimo Indian Store building, which actually has its own exit off Interstate 40. Visitors can see the World's Largest Petrified Log, weighing in at 89,000 pounds.

Otis Baird served as deputy sheriff for Navajo County while he was running his Apache Fort trading post. Inside was a collection of snakes and a pet mountain lion. Otis would drop rattlesnakes into the jewelry cases at night in case of a break in. He sold to Paul Hatch in 1973, and the fort burned down in 1984.

The Hopi Village Indian Store and Café became Howdy Hank's Trading Post. Hank left town under lurid circumstances, selling to V. P. Richards, who later sold to Max Ortega. Ortega renamed it the Sitting Bull Trading Post. It is now the Historic Route 66 Hay Sales and Feed Store. A cartoon Howdy Hank has been repainted on the building.

Mormons settled Joseph City in 1876. Glenn Blansett and his sons built the Pacific Motel in 1947. A gas station was added, and the motel grew to 21 units. Glenn moved to lease the Jack Rabbit Trading Post in 1961, and he bought it in 1967. The station is now Heritage Glass at 4500 Main Street, and the motel units are now a storage business.

Scout, trapper, prospector, and poet Frederick "San Diego" Rawson established San Diego's Old Frontier Trading Post in 1927. He sold in 1947, and the business was awarded to Ella Blackwell in a 1955 divorce settlement. Ella had mental problems, talking to mannequins and claiming the post was established in 1873. Ella's Frontier was abandoned when she died in 1984.

This landmark was originally a Santa Fe Railroad building and then the Arizona Herpetorium. In 1949, Jack Taylor let the snakes loose and opened the Jack Rabbit Trading Post. Glenn Blansett leased it in 1961. Blansett bought it in 1967, as he retired from the state senate. His daughter and son-in-law took over in 1969. They sold the Jack Rabbit to their daughter and son-in-law, Cynthia and Antonio Jaquez, in 1995.

Billboards featuring a black bunny on a yellow background made the Jack Rabbit an icon. Taylor teamed with Wayne Troutner of the Store for Men in Winslow to erect billboards for their businesses as far away as New York. The wooden billboard blaring "here it is" across from the trading post is the 1949 original.

This stone-pillared sign welcomed Route 66 travelers to Winslow. It promoted the Hopi Snake Dance, described as the "most spectacular religious rite in the world." A caravan sponsored by the chamber of commerce left Winslow on the morning of each dance at the Hopi Villages. The altered sign still stands today.

Billed as "Winslow's Newest and Finest" in 1958, the 45-room Knotty Pines Motel, at 1500 East Third Street, had pine paneling in each unit. It was owned by Ralph and Virginia Miller with Ruth and Bill Martin. Note the fierce bear standing guard in front of the Bear Den Cocktail Lounge. P. T.'s Bar occupies this site today.

John B. Drumm came to Winslow to open a barbershop in 1889. He opened his 20-unit auto court two blocks from the center of town in 1937 and ran it until 1944. John served seven terms as justice of the peace. His wife, Frona Parr Drumm, was Winslow's first female insurance agent. The Drumm family also owned a mortuary.

The Desert Sun Motel, at 1000 East Third Street, was constructed in 1953. It advertised 33 "Comfortable and attractive air conditioned units with the finest furnishings. Free radio available and away from railroad noise." As of 2010, the Desert Sun Motel is still in business across from the Falcon Restaurant.

Jim, George, and Pete Kretsedemas emigrated from Greece to join an uncle at the Falcon Restaurant, which opened on July 9, 1955. The brothers would run the restaurant at 1113 West Third Street for the next 43 years. The Falcon, which actor Richard Burton once said had the best food between Hollywood and Kansas, is still in business.

In the 1940s, Lee Elzey built the 16-unit 66 Motor Court for Adam Mace next to Elzey's tire shop at 1102 East Second Street. Elzey had taken the motor court over completely by 1950. He renamed it the L-Z Court. The motel was later expanded to 28 units and became the L-Z Budget Motel. It was still standing but boarded up as of 2010.

The La Siesta Motel No. 2 at 911 East Second Street consisted of 23 units. It was owned by Mr. and Mrs. E. R. Crozier at the time of this view. Other owners included Mr. and Mrs. John Poeth and Mr. and Mrs. Lyle Douglass. Duncan Hines recommended the La Siesta, described by AAA in 1954 as "A pleasing motel with some large family units."

A sign featuring a giant angel welcomed travelers at Gabrielle's Kitchen on Second Street. Owned by Mr. and Mrs. W. H. Hunt, Gabrielle's advertised "Good Home Cooking" along with "Real Home Made Pies" and the "Best Coffee on Hi-Way No. 66." It was known as Gabrielle's Pancake House during the 1960s and 1970s, and the building now houses a Chinese restaurant. (Mike Ward.)

BEACON MOTEL
HIGHWAY 66, WINSLOW, ARIZ.

In 1957, AAA described the 10-unit Motel Beacon, at 600 East Second Street, as "a modest motel." Their motto was "Comfort for you." This card noted that the Beacon had "ten air conditioned units, tile baths, carpeted floors, easy chairs, reading lights and first class beds." The Beacon was later expanded to 14 units and painted lime green. The site is now occupied by a storage business and auto service firm.

The Marble Motel, at 512 East Third Street, was built in the 1940s. The motel was remodeled and a new facade was added in 1952. It is now Earl's Motor Court, operated by Lee and Floranel Earl. They advertise "sleeping on the corner in Winslow, Arizona" at the oldest Route 66 motel still operating in Winslow.

La Posada was the last of the great Fred Harvey hotels to be constructed, opening in 1930 and designed by Mary Colter. The Harvey Restaurant closed in 1956, and the hotel closed on January 15, 1959. Gutted and used as offices by the Santa Fe, it was nearly torn down. Allan Affeldt and his wife, Tina Mion, began restoration in 1997.

This view looks west on Second Street approaching Kinsley Street. Standin' on the Corner Park now occupies the site of Winslow Drugs and J.C. Penney on the far left. The park features a two-story mural by John Pugh and a life-size sculpture of a musician by Ron Adamson illustrating the Eagles song "Take It Easy." The mural was saved when the old J.C. Penney building burned on October 18, 2004.

Wayne Lowell Troutner established a dry cleaning plant in 1942, delivering laundry to other towns by plane. He later moved the cleaners to the back and opened a western wear store, the Store for Men. Charley Holmes designed the curvaceous cowgirl that adorned the sign and hundreds of billboards. Troutner sold in 1990, and the building later burned. (Old Trails Museum.)

Route 66 originally followed Second Street, past the Star Court, which later became the Starlite Motel. In 1951, Second Street became one-way eastbound, and westbound traffic was shifted to Third Street, making Winslow the first community in Arizona to establish one-way highway traffic. Interstate 40 bypassing Winslow opened on October 9, 1979.

Grover Cleveland Bazell was a lawyer and newspaper owner who opened a garage and a Buick dealership in 1921. The cabins at the Bazell Modern Camp were later connected, and it became the Bazell Modern Court, operated by Mr. and Mrs. Robert Powell. Some of the structures still stand and are used as private residences.

The Entré Restaurant and Cocktail Lounge opened in 1958 and is still in business today at 1919 West Second Street. It was operated by Steve and Helen Sponduris, who were married in a big Greek wedding at the restaurant in 1961. In 1962, the Entré opened the Carnival Room, advertising Winslow's first *Bierstube* (beer hall).

Four

METEOR CITY TO WINONA

Former Hawaiian bandleader Ray Meany and his wife, Ella Blackwell, owned the Hopi House at Route 66 and Arizona Route 99, known as Leupp Corner. They also owned the Old Frontier in Joseph City. When they divorced, Ella got the Old Frontier and Ray swapped the Hopi House for a motel in California. Interstate 40 doomed the Hopi House.

Winslow was promoted as "Meteor City," and Joseph Sharber took the name for his service station, constructed in 1938. Jack Newsum took over the station in 1941, opened a trading post, and erected a sign on Route 66 reading "Meteor City—Population 1." Jack is shown here with his wife, Gloria, having changed the sign to read "Population 2" after they were married in 1946. (Old Trails Museum.)

Jack and Gloria Newsum are posed in front of the original Meteor City Trading Post. Jack died in 1960, and Gloria became known as "The Witch of Route 66" for handing down harsh speeding fines as justice of the peace. This building burned in the 1960s. Since 1979, the trading post has been housed in a geodesic dome. (Old Trails Museum.)

Meteor City was featured in the 1984 film *Starman*, starring Jeff Bridges. A new dome was erected after a fire in 1990. Dan and Judi Kempton took over in 1989 but closed down in 2001. In 2002, Richard and Emelia Benton revived Meteor City. The post is home to the world's longest map of Route 66, restored in 2003. (Library of Congress.)

Hopi Indians believed this massive crater was caused by a god who was cast from heaven. It was discovered by the white man in 1871 and at the time was believed to have been of volcanic origin. Meteor Crater is 4,150 feet across, 3 miles around the top, and 570 feet deep. The rim rises more than 150 feet above the surrounding desert.

Philadelphia mining engineer Daniel Moureau Barringer set up mining equipment at the crater in 1903. Barringer was ridiculed when he said the crater was caused by a meteor. He spent the rest of his life and much of his private capital searching for the meteor, finding only fragments. Barringer's theory was accepted after he died in 1929.

Harry Locke was interested in Dr. Barringer's work and owned the land where Route 66 met the road to the crater. Harry and his wife, Hope, operated a service station at the spot they called Meteor Junction. Locke became well known for cartoon postcards such as this one, all the while dreaming of building a meteor museum.

To raise money for their dream, the Lockes leased Meteor Station to the colorful "Rimmy Jim" Giddings (at right) in August 1933. Giddings erected signs saying he kept a graveyard for salesmen and placed an intercom beneath the outhouse seats to startle unsuspecting travelers. Giddings died in 1943. Ruth and Sid Griffin would run Rimmy Jim's until Interstate 40 came through.

Harry Locke's Meteor Crater Observatory opened in the late 1930s but failed to make money and was lost to foreclosure. Locke developed a comic strip called *Desert Cuties* and was gaining acclaim when he agreed to help out the short-handed Winslow Police Department. He died at age 56 after battling a drunk prisoner. Dr. Harvey Nininger took over the observatory, opening the American Meteorite Museum on October 19, 1946.

Dr. Harvey Nininger's American Meteorite Museum attracted 33,000 visitors in the first year and became a renowned center for research. It housed about 5,000 meteorites, the largest collection of any institution at the time. But Route 66 was moved to the north in 1949, and museum closed in 1953. The crumbling ruins remain today.

A town "wilder than Tombstone" sprouted when construction of the Atlantic and Pacific Railroad was halted at Canyon Diablo due to financial difficulties in 1881–1882. Canyon Diablo's Hell Street was lined with 14 saloons, 10 gambling dens, and 4 brothels. The first marshal was killed five hours after being sworn in, and only one lawman survived as long as 30 days. The town died when this bridge was finished. (National Archives.)

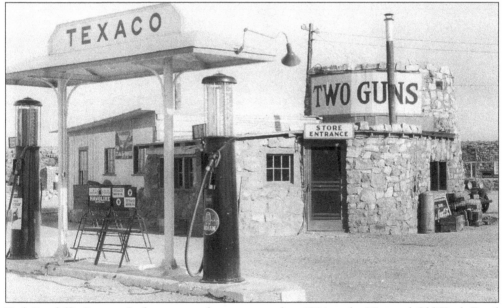

Earl Cundiff's Canyon Lodge store and camp opened in 1924 at the National Old Trails Road Bridge over Canyon Diablo. In March 1925, he leased it to the mystical Harry "Indian" Miller. Miller had lived among the Philippine headhunters and worked in silent films. Billing himself as "Chief Crazy Thunder," he built a roadside zoo and named the complex Fort Two Guns after a film starring his pal William S. Hart.

In 1878, Navajos trapped 42 murderous Apaches in a cave near Canyon Diablo, filled the entrance with brush, and set it on fire. The Apaches died horribly. Harry Miller built fake ruins and made the "Apache Death Cave" part of his roadside attraction. In 1926, Miller shot and killed his landlord, Earl Marion Cundiff. Cundiff was unarmed, but Miller claimed self-defense and was acquitted. (Phil Gordon.)

This view shows the roadside zoo at Two Guns. Harry Miller was never forgiven by some locals for shooting Earl Cundiff. Miller was also convicted of defacing Cundiff's tombstone, which read "Killed by Indian Miller." Facing more legal troubles, Miller left in 1930 to open another business at the Cave of the Seven Devils, on Route 66 at the New Mexico–Arizona state line.

Louise Cundiff, Earl's widow, married Phillip Hesch in 1934. Route 66 was relocated in 1938, and Hesch constructed this store, station, and residence. He reestablished the zoo behind the store. Benjamin Dreher built a modern motel and station at Two Guns in 1963 that burned spectacularly in 1971. Only ghostly ruins remain at Two Guns today.

The Toonerville Trading Post was one of six trading posts on Route 66 between Winslow and Winona. Earl Tinnin ran the businesses at Two Guns from 1933 to 1935 before opening Toonerville. He sold in 1954. Owner Daniel "Slick" McAlister was killed in a robbery here on August 30, 1971. The building was converted to a private home and still stands. (Phil Gordon.)

The Canyon Padre Trading Post became the Twin Arrows Trading Post in 1954. Jean and William Troxell ran it from 1955 to 1985. Two giant arrows made from utility poles out front made Twin Arrows famous. It closed in the late 1990s, but the arrows have been restored. The Hopi tribe plans to renovate the buildings for an "Indian Marketplace."

Winona is not really a town but gets a mention in the song "(Get Your Kicks on) Route 66" because it rhymes with Arizona. It actually lies 18 miles east of Flagstaff and is listed out of sequence in the song. Billy Adams built the Winona Trading Post in 1924, and his wife, Myrtle, became the state's first female postmaster. Adams added a 14-unit motel in 1925 and built a new trading post when Route 66 was realigned in the 1950s.

Five

FLAGSTAFF

Gibson's "Chix Fry" (C H I X)
3 miles East of Flagstaff, Arizona
On U. S. Highway '66' and '89'

Ira, Helen, and Jerry Gibson opened Gibson's Chix Fry east of Flagstaff in 1945 offering "one-half unjointed fried chicken, shoe string potatoes, and bread in a wax lined box." The Gibsons invited patrons to "visit our Broiler Plant and Butcher Shop." It became Kenney's Chix Fry in 1960 and was in business into the mid-1960s.

W. W. and Lucretia Sample opened Camp Elden in 1934. W. W. Sample and his brother started the Red Bluff gas station chain, which grew to include locations across Arizona on Route 66. Lucretia Sample would not allow liquor to be sold, but a liquor store opened here after they sold in 1945. Note that gas was selling for 19¢ per gallon. (Michael Luke.)

Starlite Lanes at 3406 East Santa Fe Avenue opened on November 9, 1957. They advertised "16 lanes, AMF Automatic Pinspotters, AMF Tele-Scores, underground ball returns, luxurious cocktail lounge and a free baby sitting room with a capable attendant on duty." Starlite Lanes is still in business today.

56

Taxidermist and sportsman Dean Eldredge built a log cabin around five huge ponderosa pines to display his collection of 30,000 mounts and oddities. "The Zoo," as it was known by locals, opened on June 20, 1931. Doc Williams turned it into a nightclub in 1936, after Eldredge died and the collection was sold off. Don Scott, who played with Bob Wills and the Texas Playboys, made the old museum a country music showcase in the 1960s.

Don Scott's wife, Thorna, died after falling down the stairs at the Museum Club in 1973. Shattered, Don took his own life two years later. Their ghosts are said to haunt the club. Martin and Stacie Zanzucchi ran the Museum Club from 1978 until 2005. Now operated by Joe and Shannyn Lange, the club is one of the best-known roadhouses on Route 66.

El Pueblo Motor Inn
"In the Heart of the Old West"
On U. S. Highway '66' and '89'
3 miles East of Flagstaff, Arizona

Phillip Johnston saved an untold number of lives during World War II. Raised among the Navajos, he developed a code based on their complex, unwritten language. The Navajo "Code Talkers" served in every Marine assault in the Pacific from 1942 to 1945. E. B. Goble built El Pueblo Motel for Johnston in 1936. It still stands today.

Seven motels were constructed in Flagstaff during 1963, including the Pony Soldier Motel at 3030 East Santa Fe Avenue. The 90-unit Pony Soldier advertised the "Largest Pool in Northern Arizona." It was operated by Paul Greer until 1977 and then by Doris and Joseph Childers. The motel is now the Best Western Pony Soldier Inn and Suites.

Joe and Lila Lockhard, her sons Howard and Bob Leonard, and Bob's wife, Norma, bought a motel, station, and Trixie's Diner in 1942. They named the motel the L and L and planned to call the café the Let's Eat. But Bob's uncle said it needed a zippier name. Miz Zip's, with "Let's Eat" in neon on the facade, is still serving locals and travelers.

Myron Wells, owner of the 66 Motel, served two terms as president of the Arizona chapter of the Route 66 Association. He led the No By-Pass Committee, a group that fought the Interstate 40 bypass and then tried to ban any new businesses on I-40 or between Route 66 and the new highway. The 66 Motel survived and is still in business today at 2100 East Santa Fe Avenue. (Mike Ward.)

ARROWHEAD LODGE - U. S. 66 and 89 - Flagstaff, Ariz.

Rex E. Goble's Auto Court at 2010 East Santa Fe Avenue became the Arrowhead Lodge after he died in 1941. In June 1959, it was remodeled into the Gaslite Motel, "With a friendly 'glow' that's difficult to leave—impossible to forget." In the 1960s, the name changed to the Twilite Motel. It is now the Arrowhead Lodge and Apartments.

"Gateway to Grand Canyon"
U.S. HIGHWAYS 66 & 89 . . . East Entrance . . . FLAGSTAFF, ARIZONA

Advertised as the "Motel with the VIEW," the Wonderland Motel opened at 2000 East Santa Fe Avenue in 1956. Owners Waldo and Adelyne Spelta advertised the 20-unit motel as "Flagstaff's Newest and Finest," with "Nature's air conditioning." It is still in business and appears to be in great shape.

Mr. and Mrs. Lester Smith opened the Frontier Motel at 1700 East Santa Fe Avenue on September 8, 1956. It originally had 26 units, later expanded to 31. It was later operated by Don Toalston, and then George and Vera Skylstead operated it from 1957 into the 1970s. The Frontier was demolished in 2008.

Harold Melville built the Western Hills Motel at 1580 East Santa Fe Avenue in 1953. Charles O. Greening owned it from 1954 to 1969. The impressive animated neon sign is the oldest in Flagstaff. A string of Thai establishments later occupied the restaurant, and Craig Chang opened the Pho Dai Loc Vietnamese Restaurant here in 2008.

Mr. and Mrs. Jack McCorhan opened the Skyline Motel on May 14, 1948, at 1526 East Santa Fe Avenue. Later owners included Mr. and Mrs. Fred G. Long, Lester Smith and his wife, and C. D. Samuel and Stan North. The Skyline originally had 22 units, later expanded to 28. It became the Red Rose Inn Motel, still in business today.

Earl Tinnin, who had constructed the Toonerville Trading Post, owned the Ben Franklin Motel at 1416 East Santa Fe Avenue. It was later owned by Mr. and Mrs. Ray Young. Ernest Castro, a Flagstaff public school teacher, and his wife, Vera, operated it from 1961 until 1976. Later the West Wind Motel, the site is now a shopping center.

This restaurant at 914 East Santa Fe Avenue was simply named the Steak House, operated for many years by Maurice and Mary Grant. It was the Pharaoh Restaurant in the 1960s and later became the Steak House again. This postcard advertises "Complete One-Stop Car Service While You Eat." The Norvel Owens Mortuary stands here today.

Flagstaff Motor Village
U.S. 66 - 89, in Town, Flagstaff, Arizona

There were 17 "modern, clean comfortable and convenient units with private garages" and a Mobil station at the Flagstaff Motor Village, 402 East Santa Fe Avenue. Gordon and Jane Beckley ran the motel for the Babbitt family from 1949 to 1969. The station was closed in 1959, and the motel site is now the Jim Babbitt Ford used car lot.

On July 4, 1876, a group of immigrants cut the limbs off a pine tree for a flag staff to celebrate the U.S. centennial. A railroad camp established in April 1880 was named Flag Staff, shortened to one word in 1881. Before construction of a railroad overpass in 1934, Route 66 turned onto Beaver Street to Phoenix Avenue and Mike's Pike.

The railroad camp was relocated a bit to the east in 1883, and "New Town" sprang up. Railroad Avenue, the future Route 66, is in the foreground in this view of New Town. At right is the Brannen General Store, the first stone building. James Vail's saloon is on the left. Between the structures is present-day San Francisco Street. (Library of Congress.)

An old boxcar served as the depot when the railroad arrived in Flagstaff on August 1, 1882. It grew to four boxcars before a stone depot was built in 1889. The Santa Fe completed a new depot just to the west in 1926. Now the Flagstaff Visitor's Center, it is of English Tudor design, with a steeply pitched roof to shed the heavy snow. (Mike Ward.)

Eddie Wong opened the Grand Canyon Café at 110 East Santa Fe Avenue in 1938. His brother Albert joined him in 1940. A 1950 expansion added the distinctive brick front, windows rounded on one side, and stainless steel canopy over the entrance. The Grand Canyon Café is still in business today, noted for its chicken fried steak.

Looking west on Santa Fe Avenue, a sign on the Vail Building points toward Edwin D. Babbitt's Ford dealership. The Commercial Hotel opened in 1888. It had the first indoor plumbing in town and was the headquarters of Western novelist Zane Grey. An arsonist destroyed the landmark on November 14, 1975, just hours after it was condemned.

The same view in 1948 shows Black's Lounge in the Vail Building, later Club 66. Jerry Midgley's Rose Tree Café was operated by Wong June Jr. into the 1950s. J. R. Cooper's Buffett replaced Joe Bender's Café. Lee Jenkins ran Wigwam Indian Curios, and Jerry Andreatos owned the El Patio Café, now the Flagstaff Brewing Company.

Photographer Frank Sofea turned to the restaurant business in 1922 when his eyesight failed. He moved his Black Cat Café to 6 East Santa Fe Avenue in the early 1930s. It later became the Out West Café. Wing Sing Gee took over in 1961 and opened the Hong Kong Restaurant. The building now houses a sushi bar.

Khatter Joseph Nackard built the Downtowner Auto Court in 1929 on the site of an old brothel on San Francisco Street. In 1933, the cabins were connected to form the Nackard Inn. Nackard ran an illegal slot machine operation, paying part of the proceeds to the chamber of commerce. The inn became the Downtowner Motel in the 1950 and is now apartments.

Albert N. Du Beau's motel was the first in Arizona to offer amenities for motorists such as garages, sheets, and steam heat. It opened at 19 West Phoenix Street, a block off Route 66, in 1929. There were 28 units with his residence and office in front. It is now the Du Beau International Hostel. Albert's daughter Clara once ran the Black Cat Café.

Salvador Esparza was a carpenter who used sandstone and fieldstone to construct his Sierra Vista Motel, which opened on May 19, 1948, at 9 East Phoenix Avenue. There were 21 units decorated in Spanish Colonial style. The large neon sign atop the Sierra Vista remained in place until a new roof was added around 2007–2008.

John Weatherford's Hotel at Aspen Avenue and Leroux Street opened on January 1, 1900. Weatherford also built the Majestic Opera House, which collapsed under 6 feet of snow on December 31, 1915. Its replacement, the Orpheum, is visible in the background. Henry Taylor and his wife, Sam, have restored the historical hotel.

City leaders held a public subscription to build a new hotel downtown that opened on January 1, 1927. A 12-year-old girl won the contest to name the hotel when she suggested Monte Vista, Spanish for "mountain view." The hotel was publicly owned until the early 1960s. The Monte Vista is the oldest continuously operating hotel in Flagstaff.

Arthur Vandevier spent 13 years enforcing the law in Coconino County, opening the Vandevier Lodge with his wife, Laura, in June 1941. It was expanded into a motel in 1953 with seven additional units and a new sign. The motel, at 402 West Santa Fe Avenue, was torn down in May 1977, and apartments were constructed on the site.

Joe L. Sharber and Haydee Lane opened the Lane Motel on February 26, 1948, at 122 West Santa Fe Avenue. In 1958, the Lanes sold the motel to Diamond Sampson, who also owned the Snow Bowl Motel. Sampson tore down the gas station. It later became the Townhouse Motel, now the Rodeway Inn Downtown.

The L Motel was operated by Mr. and Mrs. Luther L. Jones and later by Mr. and Mrs. Alvin Arntsen. In 1954, AAA described the motel as "nicely furnished" with 13 open garages. The L Motel at 121 South Sitgreaves Street (now South Milton Road) originally had 15 units, later expanded to 20, and developed into the Rodeway Inn University.

The Lumber Jack Café opened in 1961. It was originally Tony Souris's Steakhouse, which opened in 1946. Robert and Violet Morrison sold the Lumber Jack to Martin, Hank, and Matt Zanzucchi in 1974, and it became Granny's Closet Restaurant. The café's two giant lumberjacks now guard the Walkup Skydome at Northern Arizona University.

The Spur Motel, at 224 Mike's Pike, opened in 1956. It was operated by Mr. and Mrs. Chester Dohr and later by Mr. and Mrs. R. E. Leaders. In 1957, AAA described the 15-unit motel at the entrance to the university as "a very nice new motel with attractively furnished one and two room units." It is now the Knight's Inn.

Lemuel and Milton Stroud founded the small Park Plaza Motel chain, with locations on Route 66 at Flagstaff, Amarillo, Tulsa, and St. Louis. Lemuel Stroud built units in the back that served as motel rooms in the summer and as the Stroud Hall dormitory when Arizona State College, now Northern Arizona University, was in session.

The Golden Drumstick opened in 1952 next to the Park Plaza Motel. The restaurant offered a dinner of chicken, fries, and honey for $1. There were also Golden Drumstick locations in Phoenix and Tucson. George Nackard opened the Gables Restaurant and Cameo Room here on June 5, 1959. The Gables was once home to KEOS radio, and the building is now the Mandarin Supper Buffet.

This view looks west at the intersection of Route 66 and U.S. 89A. Phoenix developer Andy Womack's "Spanish western frontier style" El Rancho Motel (right) opened on December 9, 1947, and became the Flamingo Motel in 1959. It closed in 1986 and was demolished in 1997. A Barnes and Noble bookstore now occupies the site.

In 1954, Flamingo Hotels bought the El Rancho and constructed the Flamingo Motor Hotel adjoining to the west. In 1959, the Flamingo became the very first Ramada Inn. The name is Spanish for a "shady resting place," according to the company Web site. The motel at 602 West Highway 66 is now a Super Eight.

This marker stood where U.S. 89A split off from Route 66 and 89 at the west end of Flagstaff. Alternate Route 89 takes travelers to scenic Oak Creek Canyon, while Routes 66 and 89 head towards Williams. In 1992, the City of Flagstaff changed the names of parts of Santa Fe Avenue, Sitgreaves Street, and Milton Road back to Route 66.

A lumber mill had served as a landmark at the southwest entrance to Flagstaff since at least 1889. The Saginaw and Manistee Lumber Company operated this mill from 1941 until it was sold and closed down in 1954. A fire set as a high school graduation prank destroyed the landmark on May 29, 1961.

The Saga Motel at 820 West Highway 66 opened in August 1961 and was operated by Barbara and Ray Larkey. The 29-unit motel was later owned by Edward J. Canepa, a Flagstaff civic leader who died in 1973. It is now the Saga Budget Host Inn, and the beautiful blinking blue neon name on the facade remains.

Mr. and Mrs. Jack McCorhan also owned the 29-unit Branding Iron Motel and Dining Room at 1121 West Highway 66. It advertised "Rest away from R.R. Noise" and "Unsurpassed Motel accommodations and fine eating. You'll enjoy the friendly western hospitality and the wonderful mountain air." The site is now a car lot.

The San Francisco Peaks are sacred to many American Indian tribes. The Hopi believed they were the home of the Kachina spirits. There are six peaks, Agassiz, Aubineau, Doyle, Fremont, Humphreys, and Rees. Humphreys Peak is the highest point in Arizona at 12,633 feet. It was named for the general in charge of the early surveyor data. (Mike Ward.)

Six

PARKS TO WILLIAMS

In November 1921, Art Anderson and Don McMillan's store and station opened where the National Old Trails Highway met the road to the Grand Canyon. It is now the Parks in the Pines General Store. The transcontinental Bunion Derby runners passed the store in March 1928. The eventual winner, Andy Payne, is at left. (Kaibab Forest Service.)

Most visitors to the Grand Canyon originally traveled by rail. The first bumpy automobile road from Flagstaff to the canyon opened in 1900. The National Park Service began construction on a good highway in 1928, and it was paved within a few years. This view shows the turn-off from Route 66 between Flagstaff and Williams.

The McHat Inn, located 8 miles east of Williams, became the Wagon Wheel Lodge, operated by Gordon and Juanita McDowell from 1936 to 1959. McDowell was a respected businessman and served on the Coconino County Board of Supervisors. But with the Elmo Dance Hall across the road, the lodge gained a reputation as a brothel during the 1940s. The log building still stands and is now a private residence.

KAIBAB MOTOR LODGE
WILLIAMS, ARIZONA

Mr. and Mrs. Lee Treece ran the 18-unit Kaibab Motor Lodge, 100 yards off Route 66 and "Away from Traffic Noise." It later became the Canyon Motel, which Kevin and Shirley Young converted into the Canyon Hotel and RV Park. Travelers today can sleep in a 1929 Santa Fe Railroad caboose or one of the restored flagstone motel units.

Grand Canyon Court and Station
At Underpass, Williams, Arizona
On U. S. Highway '66'

Originally Route 66 made sharp turns and crossed the railroad at grade entering Williams, where Hubert Clark first operated his camp. He built the Grand Canyon Court and Station when an underpass was built in 1932. Clark was a booster of aviation, and the local airport was named in his honor in 1992. Later operated by Harvey Gibbs, the 42 cabins in the pines were demolished in the 1950s for the Thunderbird Inn.

The Thunderbird Inn at 642 East Bill Williams Avenue opened in 1957 and advertised as "The most complete stop on Route 66." It offered 96 luxurious rooms, with a swimming pool, gift shop, restaurant, and cocktail lounge. The Thunderbird became the Mountainside Inn and Conference Center.

In 1958, AAA recommended the new 18-unit El Rancho Motel as "very attractive and well maintained." It advertised "Tubs and Showers in Every Room" and was "Beautifully Furnished." Two more units were later added to the two-story brick motel. The El Rancho is still in business at 617 East Bill Williams Avenue.

C. C. Cheshire ran an auto dealership on West Santa Fe Avenue at Sitgreaves Street in Flagstaff. His brother-in-law A. T. Davis Jr. operated this Cheshire Motors location in Williams at 520 East Bill Williams Avenue. This structure is now occupied by Import Auto Service, but the "Chevrolet" and "Buick" lettering on the smokestack is still visible.

Mr. and Mrs. Lee Treece operated the El Coronado Motel. It originally had 27 rooms, expanded to 42 by the time this view was taken. Located across from Rod's Famous Steak House, the El Coronado offered special day rates for tourists planning to drive across the desert at night. It is now the EconoLodge.

Williams Motel
"The Gateway to Grand Canyon"
U.S. 66 - 89, Williams, Arizona

Dorothy and Dick Boyack's Williams Motel was located next door to Rod's Steak House. It originally consisted of 16 units. An additional structure was later added, bringing the total to 28. Wild West Junction, home of the largest collection of John Wayne memorabilia outside the Wayne family, now occupies this site.

Rodney Graves organized the city's first rodeo and was one of the founders of the Bill Williams Mountain Men. Rod's Steak House opened on August 23, 1946. Graves retired in 1967. In 1985, Stella and Lawrence Sanchez took over the landmark. The sign features Domino the cow, and the souvenir menus are shaped like Domino.

The Del Sue Motel was originally a "Traveler's Tent Camp" in the 1920s. The motel was the first in Williams and opened in 1936. Sue Delaney operated the Del Sue, which is now the Grand Motel. The recently refurbished motel at 234 East Bill Williams Avenue is listed on the National Register of Historic Places.

Roy and Grace Gamble invited travelers to "Enjoy a Night of Rest among the Pines" at the Gateway Motel. They advertised "clean units, all modern, four good restaurants within one-half block." Constructed in 1936, it is now an office plaza, and the former office is now J. D.'s Espresso. Fortunately the sign was preserved.

Everett and Laverne Coffee owned the Mount Williams Motor Court and expanded it into the 16-unit Downtowner Motel. When Route 66 through Williams was divided, part of the back row of units was removed for a driveway to the westbound lanes. It is now the Rodeway Inn and Suites Downtowner Motel at 201 East Bill Williams Avenue.

The Sun Dial Motel at 200 East Bill Williams Avenue was owned by J. H. Venable and later operated by Doc and Bea Starkey. It advertised "nicely furnished, fully carpeted units with tubs and showers, in the tall pine country of Northern Arizona." Renovated in 2003, it is now known as The Lodge.

Starky's Motel

Williams, Arizona

In the Heart of Town on U. S. Highways 66-89

Originally Bethel's Tourist Court, Starky's Motel was notable for the angled buttresses protruding from the front. Mike "Starky" Starkovich advertised "Ten attractively furnished units." The buttresses are gone, but the motel still stands. It is now the Royal American Inn, at 134 East Bill Williams Avenue.

Hull's Motel Inn was operated by Mr. and Mrs. D. A. Hosack. John and Myrtle Smart bought the 12-cottage motel in the 1940s. The cottages were connected to form 17 units with enclosed garages, and it became Hull's Motel. John died in 1947, and Myrtle ran it until 1958. The motel at 128 Bill Williams Avenue is now the Historic Route 66 Inn.

The Coffee Pot Café (at left) was operated by Mr. and Mrs. John Mills and later by Mr. and Mrs. J. W. Duffield. They advertised "The Best Coffee in Town." The souvenir menus were printed in the shape of a coffee pot. This building now houses the Native America Shop at 117 East Bill Williams Avenue.

On September 17, 1901, Williams became the "Gateway to the Grand Canyon," when the Santa Fe Railroad began service to the natural wonder. The Fray Marcos de Niza Hotel was completed in 1908. The Fred Harvey Company ran the restaurant. The ticket office closed in 1954. In 1989, the Grand Canyon Railway restored the structure to serve as the depot for its steam train excursions to the canyon.

In 1955, Route 66 was divided through Williams. Bill Williams Avenue carried eastbound Route 66, and westbound traffic used Railroad Avenue. Williams was the last community on Route 66 to be bypassed. Bobby Troup sang his "(Get Your Kicks On) Route 66" during the bittersweet ceremony when Interstate 40 opened on October 13, 1984.

August Tetzlaff built this saloon, tailor shop, and bordello on "Whiskey Row" across from the depot in 1897. It was later owned by Longino Moro, who married five times and had 25 children. He is second from left in this view, next to the house madam toting a pistol. The brothel and saloon closed after a murder in the 1940s. Restored by John Holst, the building now houses the Red Garter Bed and Breakfast. (John Holst.)

The Pollock Building, at left, originally had one story and was built with volcanic rock in 1901. Jewell Vaughn and her husband, Reese, operated Vaughn's Indian Store here from 1937 to 1941. They sold to Bernice Montgomery in 1941, and she married Frank Irwin in 1953. The Irwins sold the business to Melvin and Madene Beddo in 1962. The store was moved to a more modern one-story location, shown on page 86.

This view looks east on Bill Williams Avenue from Fourth Street. The original location of Mill's Café housed *Route 66 Magazine* from 1997 to 2001 and is now the Java Cycle Coffee House. In 1908, the pioneering Babbitt brothers of Flagstaff opened a general store with Gus and F. O. Polson. It grew into Babbitt's Department Store, at right.

By the 1950s, Bill Lee's Café occupied the original Mill's Café location. The Mill's had moved to the old Arnold's Café site in the Pollock Building. Sutton's Court, at right, was later a Whiting Brothers Motel and is now the Arizona 9 Motor Hotel. The Sultana Theatre is also on the right. It opened in 1912, originally showing silent movies.

Williams was founded in 1876 and named for William Sherley Williams, a famous trapper and scout of the Santa Fe Trail. The Bill Williams Mountain Men, shown here on parade through town, were founded in 1953 to honor the pioneer trappers and traders. They ride to Phoenix on horseback each year to teach youths about history and have participated in several presidential inaugural parades.

The Westerner Motel, at 530 West Bill Williams Avenue, was owned and managed by Mr. and Mrs. Ray Stewart and later by Melvin and Madene Beddo. The 10-unit motel advertised "Gyramatic Mattresses" and was described by AAA as "a pleasant motel." The Westerner is still in business today.

The rooms were "Air Conditioned by Nature," and they offered "separate dressing rooms" at the 12-unit Highlander Motel. Owners included Marshall and Ruth Ann Duncan as well as Marion and "Whitey" Christensen. The refurbished motel at 533 West Route 66 now advertises, "We may be small, but we will do our best to make you smile."

In 1946, Rodney Graves, who also ran Rod's Steak House, opened Old Smoky's Pancake House and Restaurant, constructed with flat stone very similar to the "giraffe rock" used in the Missouri Ozarks. Mr. and Mrs. Miles Cureton took over in 1952. Elvis Presley once ate here, and Old Smoky's is little changed today.

Norris and Harold Hanson's firm constructed the Norris Motel at 1001 West Highway 66. Opened in 1953, it advertised 16 "distinctively designed units." The Norris was operated by Marion and Reese Morgan, then by L. M. Thompson and George Wyatt, and later by Vern and Fran Thompson. It is now the Best Value Inn.

Harvey J. Gibbs, former owner of Grand Canyon Camp, opened Harvey's Hacienda at the west end of Williams. Max and Pauline Andrews were running it when this view was made. The complex included a 38-unit motel, a coffee shop, a dining room, a curio shop, and a cocktail lounge. The trophies awarded to the Bill Williams Mountain Men were displayed here. The Hacienda no longer stands.

Ashfork Hill, west of Williams, is one of the steepest sections on all of Route 66. Westbound motorists drop about 1,700 feet over 7 miles. The original highway, with its twists and blind crests, was a terror for tourists and truckers alike, especially when traffic increased after World War II. The final section of new highway taming the hill opened in July 1954.

Seven

ASHFORK TO KINGMAN

In 1928, Ezell and Zelma Nelson opened the Copper State Modern Cottages in Ashfork, later the Copper State Court. Ezell built 12 cottages of cobblestone with walls 18 inches thick. The garages had railings inside for tying up horses. The Nelsons operated the Copper State Court until 1975. George and Brenda Bannister bought it in 1989.

The first Harvey House in Ashfork was a wooden structure that burned in 1905. It was replaced by the beautifully landscaped and luxurious Escalante, named after explorer Silvestre Escalante. The hotel closed in 1951, and the restaurant closed in 1953. Local citizens tried to save it, but the landmark was torn down in 1968.

Looking west, Frank Gum's Buffett, the White House Hotel, Arizona Hotel, and 66 Café are at left. At right are McMahan's Texaco, O'Brien's Shamrock Café, Gorra's Pool Hall and Bar, and Joe Gang's Arizona Café and Bar. The Arizona Café building is one of the few structures remaining from the glory days of Route 66, and it is now a church.

Ashfork was a busy place before the Santa Fe Railroad moved the mainline away in 1950. The opening of Interstate 40 in 1979 was another devastating blow. A fire on November 20, 1977, and another on October 7, 1987, virtually wiped out the business district. The quiet town today boasts of being the "Flagstone Capital of the World." (Mike Ward.)

The Hi-Line Modern Auto Court, "Your Home Away From Home," opened in 1936 and was owned by Alton McAbee. It was later owned and operated by Mr. and Mrs. J. R. Edwards. It became the Hi-Line Motel in the 1950s. At that time, a Shell station in the center of the complex was converted to the office and residence.

Joe and Edie DeSoto turned an old Texaco station into DeSoto's Beauty and Barbershop. A 1960 Chrysler DeSoto with "Elvis" at the wheel is perched on the roof. During the glory years of Route 66, the Green Door Bar was located in the building at left, now the Route 66 Grill. It was also known for a time as the Crow Bar. (Library of Congress.)

The longest remaining unbroken stretch of Route 66 begins at Exit 139 on Interstate 40 between Ashfork and Seligman and runs 162 miles to Topock. Seligman was originally known as Prescott Junction, founded in 1886 and later renamed for railroad financier Jesse Seligman. Interstate 40 opened on September 22, 1978, but the town refused to die.

96

The Bil-Mar-Den Motel had 44 units and was featured in a Ford commercial in the 1960s. Now the Stagecoach 66 Motel, the awesome sign is still in use. Seligman served as inspiration for the fictional town of Radiator Springs in the movie *Cars*. The community's preserved Route 66 heritage now makes it a popular tourist stop.

The Supai Motel at 134 East Chino Avenue opened in 1952 and takes its name from the nearby Havasupai Reservation. Advertised as "Seligman's newest and finest," it was owned and operated by Mr. and Mrs. H. Lanier and later by Mr. and Mrs. C. Van Ausdall. The renovated 15-room motel and its vintage sign still welcome travelers.

In 1953, Juan Delgadillo salvaged material from the railroad and built his drive-in with help from his brothers and father. Turned down by Dairy Queen, Juan signed with the Sno Cap chain. He delighted tourists with a menu offering "Dead Chicken," fake door handles, and a mustard bottle that squirted yellow string. Juan died on June 2, 2004. His family carries on the tradition. (Library of Congress.)

Angel Delgadillo opened a barbershop in his dad's old pool hall on May 22, 1950, and moved a few blocks to this location in 1972. Angel spearheaded the formation of the Historic Route 66 Association of Arizona in 1987, which started the Route 66 revival. Angel and his wife, Vilma, operate the Route 66 Gift Shop and Visitor's Center.

The Court De Luxe was constructed in 1932 and is now the De Luxe Inn, the oldest motel still in operation in Seligman. Advertised as "new and fireproof," and "quiet, restful, attractively furnished," the Court De Luxe also offered closed garages and steam-heated rooms with or without tub or shower baths at "popular prices."

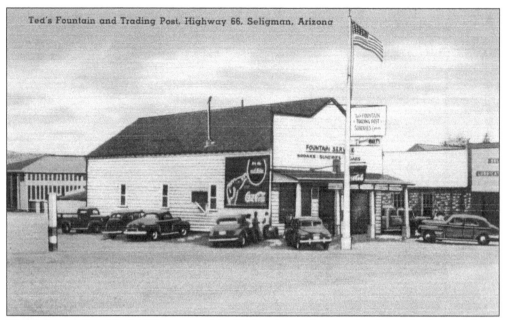

The Seligman Sundries building opened in 1904 and over the years has housed a theater, dance hall, and Ted's Trading Post and Soda Fountain. At one time, the building had the only telephone in Seligman. During the 1920s, cowboy actor Tom Mix stopped here. The building now houses Route 66 Historic Seligman Sundries.

The Havasu in Seligman was one of six Harvey Hotels in Arizona. It opened around 1905 and was named after the Havasupai tribe. It closed in 1954 and was used as offices by the Santa Fe before being abandoned and gutted. It was demolished in April 2008. The reading room now serves as a biology building at Seligman High School. (Mike Ward.)

Ethel Rutherford and her husband, who ran the Qumacho Café and Inn, opened the Copper Cart Restaurant in 1950. Louise Brown kept it going after Interstate 40 arrived. In February 1987, Angel Delgadillo called a meeting here that resulted in the organization of the Historic Route 66 Association of Arizona. The Copper Cart closed in 2008 but was remodeled and reopened a few months later.

Signs advertising the Hyde Park tourist camp west of Seligman invited travelers to "Park Your Hide at Hyde Park." For decades, Hyde Park offered the closest accommodations to Yampai/ Coconino Caverns and was marked on road maps. Only the foundations of some buildings and a debris-filled swimming pool remain today. (Phillip Gordon.)

In 1927, Walter Peck was on his way to a poker game when he stumbled and nearly fell into a deep cave entrance. Peck used a winch to lower tourists into the cave, known as Yampai Caverns and then Coconino Caverns. A staircase was built in 1936. The name was changed to Dinosaur Caverns in 1957 and Grand Canyon Caverns in 1962.

The Peach Springs Trading Post predates Route 66. Note the swastikas. To the Navajos, the ancient "whirling log" was a sacred symbol. Imposed on an arrowhead, the swastika actually appeared on Arizona state highway markers until 1942. A new cobblestone trading post opened in 1929 and now houses the Hualapai Forestry Department.

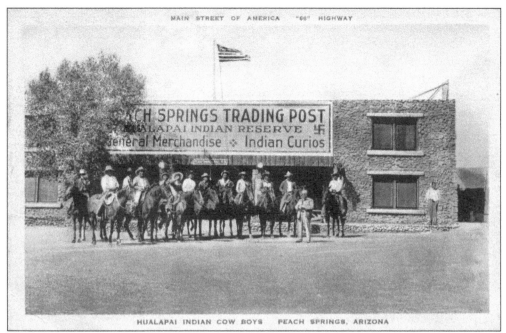

HUALAPAI INDIAN COW BOYS   PEACH SPRINGS, ARIZONA

These Hualapai cowboys posed in front of the trading post building that was constructed in 1929. Peach Springs is the headquarters of the million-acre Hualapai Reservation. Hualapai means "People of the Tall Pine." Today the tribe operates a lodge in town, and Peach Springs is the gateway to the Hualapai Grand Canyon Skywalk.

Swedish immigrant John Osterman built his station after World War I. His brother Oscar bought it in 1925 and built the structure at right when Route 66 shifted a block away in 1931. Peach Springs was devastated when Interstate 40 opened 25 miles away in 1979. But this station, later owned by Robert Goldstein, was in business until 2007.

O! C. OSTERMAN AUTO COURT — PEACH SPRINGS, ARIZONA — U.S. ROUTE 66

Oscar Osterman constructed an auto court next to his station, charging $1 for a night in a wooden shack. He later built 16 attached units. Frank and Beatrice Boyd took over in 1938, and it became the Peach Springs Auto Court. After Frank died, Beatrice continued to operate the motel into the 1980s, but the buildings have since been demolished. (Mike Ward.)

Ethel Rutherford, who later became a state representative, operated the Qumacho Café with her husband. In 1949, the café was offering the Number Seven "Cattleman's Diet" breakfast for $2.78. It consisted of six eggs (any style), half a loaf of bread (toasted), a ham steak, potatoes, and "java till the pot runs dry." (Phillip Gordon.)

During his 1857 expedition, Lt. Edward Beale named a spring Truxton, which was his mother's maiden name. Truxton was little more than a railroad watering stop until Clyde McCune opened a service station and Donald Dilts opened a café in October 1951. But like these cars, many of the businesses were abandoned when Interstate 40 opened. (Library of Congress.)

Alice Wright opened the nine-room Frontier Motel at Truxton in 1952. Mildred Barker came to work in the Frontier's café in 1955 and took over the motel with her husband, Raymond, in 1970. The sign was recently restored with help from the Route 66 Association of Arizona and the Route 66 Corridor Management Program. (Library of Congress.)

The 7-V ranch and resort along Crozier Creek at Valentine was built by Ed Carrow and his six brothers beginning in 1924. The complex grew to include a restaurant, service station, garage, and eight cabins, as well as a large swimming pool. Route 66 was relocated after a flood in 1939, but the cabins still stand. (Steve Rider.)

The Hackberry General Store was originally the Northside Grocery and closed in 1978. Artist Bob Waldmire came to the abandoned store in 1992 and established his quirky International-Bioregional Old Route 66 Visitors Center. John and Kerry Pritchard took over in 1998. The store was featured in the films *Easy Rider* and *Roadhouse 66*. (Library of Congress.)

Eight

KINGMAN TO COOL SPRINGS

In the days before auto air-conditioning, the giant flashing arrow sign blaring "Jugs Iced Free" was a welcome site for Route 66 travelers entering Kingman. The ice machine at Allen Bell's Flying A service station pumped out 450 pounds of ice cubes every day. The café was called the Tydway and was operated by Harry Tindel. (Bob Boze Bell.)

The Arizona Motel was located 3009–3023 East Andy Devine Avenue. The motel, with an attractive light turquoise brick exterior, advertised 14 modern units with tub and showers and the "Best for Less." It was owned and operated by Marjorie M. Ackerman when this view was made. The Rodeway Inn stands on this site today.

"The Very Finest Accomodations" were offered at the 25-room Pony Soldier Motel at 2939 Andy Devine Avenue. Mr. and Mrs. Tom White were the owners and operators at the time of this view. Advertised as the "Choicest Location in Kingman," it became the Route 66 Motel. The flashing arrow portion of the sign is still in use.

Bell's Motel, at 2030 East Andy Devine Avenue, was owned by Mr. and Mrs. Elza Bell. Other owners included Mr. and Mrs. Walter Beddow and Mr. and Mrs. James L. Richardson. Bell's Motel advertised "A fully modern, fire-proof, air-cooled motel." There were 13 units, and it still stands as the Desert Lodge Apartments.

The Hillcrest Motel, at 2018 Andy Devine Avenue, is still serving travelers today. AAA called it a "modest" court. It was advertised as "a new, fully modern, air-cooled motel with tile showers and electric heat" and consisted of 16 units. Owners included Earl and Ruth Chambers as well as Arlow and Gen Lamb.

City Cafe and Texaco Station, Kingman, Arizona

Roy Walker opened the City Café in 1943. William McCasland took over on March 5, 1945, and ran it for many years. The Texaco station was demolished when Andy Devine Avenue was widened. The City Café became the Hot Rod Café, but the building was torn down in 2009 to make room for a Walgreen's.

The Siesta Motel, at 1926 East Andy Devine Avenue, opened in 1929. Note the sign featuring a stereotypical image of a Mexican dozing beneath a cactus. The Siesta was operated by Mr. and Mrs. H. D. Wilbanks and was located across from the City Café. It is now the Siesta Apartments and Kitchenettes.

The Hilltop Motel at 1901 East Andy Devine Avenue advertised the "Best View in Kingman," overlooking the Hualapai Mountains. The 28-unit motel opened in 1954 and was operated by Jack and Erma Horner, later by Eleanor and George Allan, and by Louis and Charles Picard. The Hilltop Motel is still in business today.

John F. Miller knew a good deal when he saw one. In 1905, he bought a lot at First Street and Fremont Street in the dusty, isolated town of Las Vegas, Nevada. That site became Nevada Hotel, then the Hotel Sal Sagev (Las Vegas spelled backwards), and finally it grew into the Golden Gate Casino. When Hoover Dam was completed, Miller looked for Kingman to become an important crossroads, so he built the El Trovatore Motel in 1939.

After passing the Hilltop and El Trovatore Motels, Route 66/Andy Devine Avenue makes a steep descent through a rock cut into the Kingman business district. The TraveLodge chain operated a 32-unit motel at the bottom of the cut. It was later expanded to 38 rooms and is now operating as the Rambling Rose Motel.

The Brandin' Iron Motor Motel, later the Brandin' Iron Motel, was opened in 1953 by Mr. and Mrs. R. A. Bewley. Later owners included Mr. and Mrs. N. T. Gaylor and Hulan and Dixie Crawford. Advertised as "Kingman's Newest and Finest" when this view was made, the Branding Iron was demolished in 2001, and apartments were constructed on the site.

112

Charlie Lum came to Kingman from China in 1922 to work for his father at the White House Café. In 1951, he opened the Jade Restaurant and Cocktail Lounge, which he called the "Pride of Route 66." Charlie became a well-respected community leader, owning several other businesses. The vacant building still stands.

In 1938, the Arcadia Court opened at 909 Andy Devine Boulevard. Advertisements said it had the "finest appointments for the fastidious guest" and that Kingman has the "healthiest climate—no humidity and purest water." It grew to include 47 units. Frank and Susan Brace took over in 2001 and restored the property, now the Arcadia Lodge.

Opened in the early 1930s, the Gypsy Garden Auto Court was operated by Mr. and Mrs. Arthur Jones. Between 1949 and 1951, it was extensively modernized as shown here and became the Coronado Court. Stan Marbell operated the Coronado Court in the 1950s. The site in the 700 block of Andy Devine Avenue is now a vacant lot.

The Lockwood Café opened in 1937 and served "Chicken in the Rough," one of the first franchised foods. Beverly Osborne, a Route 66 restaurateur from Oklahoma City, came up with the idea of a chicken dinner eaten without silverware. The former cafe at 711 East Andy Devine Avenue is now St. Michael's Catholic Church.

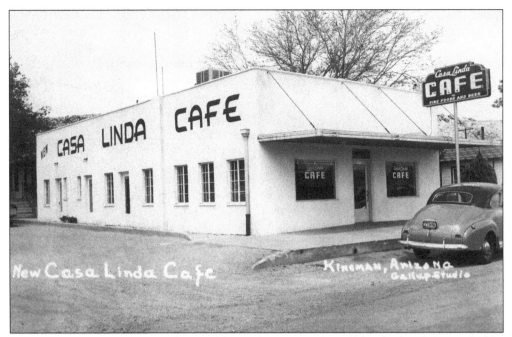

Former Harvey Girl Clara Boyd opened her café in 1933. She and her husband, Jimmy, held a contest to rename the café, offering a coffee maker to the winner. Walter "Tuffy" Spaw came up with the name Casa Linda. The Casa Linda closed in 1964, and the building at 511 East Andy Devine Avenue now houses a surveying business. (Steve Rider.)

The Wal-A-Pai Motor Court, in the 600 block of Andy Devine Avenue, took its name from the phonetic pronunciation of Hualapai and used American Indian imagery to attract tourists. This card also added "Kingman is noted for its Mountain Spring Water, we have it iced." The court, with its 40 blue and white cottages, was demolished in 2007.

Note: Sleeping Dutchman

WHITE ROCK COURT - ON HIWAY 66 - EAST END OF KINGMAN, ARIZ.

Constructed in 1935, Conrad Minka's White Rock Court was the cool place to stay. Minka drilled tunnels through solid rock into the mountain behind the motel, where he created an evaporative cooler with a water tank and burlap. Tunnels also connected the units with a central heater. Note the "Sleeping Dutchman" mountain.

Seen in this picture looking east on Front Street (now Andy Devine Avenue) at Fourth Street, the Keister's Kingman Drug Company Building was built in 1899. Lum Sing Yow's White House Café is to the right. The structures now house a restaurant. The banner promotes Kingman as educational and scenic, the "Gateway to Boulder Dam."

116

J. W. Thompson and John Mulligan built the Brunswick Hotel in 1909. They erected a wall creating two separate hotels after a dispute over a woman, whom Mulligan went on to marry. It is said to be haunted by the spirit of Mulligan's daughter, who fell down the stairs on her tricycle and died in 1920. Closed for two decades, the Brunswick was renovated in 1997, but it closed again in 2010.

The Old Trails Garage opened about 1914. Owners included Jasper Brewer, a county sheriff and state representative. During the 1920s, it advertised, "When we satisfy you we make a booster. Give us a try." A Packard repair facility was located here, and the towering sign from that era is being restored. (Jim Hinckley.)

Johanna and Harvey Hubbs ran a boardinghouse that was purchased by Thomas and Amy Devine in 1906. They renamed it the Hotel Beale in 1923, and then sold in 1926. Their son Andy Devine went on to fame as Guy Madison's sidekick in the *Wild Bill Hickok* television series. The Hotel Beale closed in 2000 and has fallen into disrepair. (Library of Congress.)

The Kimo Café and the adjoining Shell station at 105 East Andy Devine Avenue is now Mr. D'z Route 66 Diner, operated by Armando and Michelle Jimenez. Mr. D'z was in the spotlight in May 2006, when Oprah Winfrey visited and declared that the root beer was the world's best. The car is a 1940 Packard. (Jim Hinckley.)

The Desert Power and Water House, at far right, opened on July 31, 1907, and is the oldest reinforced concrete structure in Arizona. Electricity production ended in 1938. In 1997, the power house was converted into a visitor center housing an informative Route 66 museum and the Route 66 Association of Arizona's headquarters.

During World War II, over 20,000 bomber gunners trained at the Kingman Army Airfield. The airfield is shown here after the war, when it became a center for selling or scrapping thousands of military aircraft. One B-17 was sold to a Boy Scout troop for $350. The site became the Kingman Airport and Industrial Park.

Route 66 climbs into the Black Mountains west of Kingman, where N. R. Dunton ran a pipe to a spring 2 miles away and then established Cool Springs Camp in 1926. In 1936, James and Mary Walker took over and "rocked" the main building. Mary divorced James and married Floyd Slidell in 1939. The business thrived until the new highway opened in 1952.

Floyd and Mary would also be divorced, and Floyd was left to run the dying business with his niece and her husband. Cool Springs became a poultry operation called the Chicken Ranch. It was abandoned in 1964 and then burned down. Cool Springs was partly rebuilt in 1991 to be blown up for the film *Universal Soldier*. Ed Leuchtner bought it in 2002 and resurrected the landmark.

Nine

OATMAN TO TOPOCK

Prospector Lowell "Ed" Edgarton operated Ed's Camp. Tourists slept in their cars or pitched tents. One dollar rented a cot on a screened-in porch. That price also included free water, which otherwise was sold by the bucket. Ed became a well-known geologist and died in 1978. The camp and its lone saguaro cactus are still there.

Route 66 climbs 1,400 feet in 9 miles around hairpin curves with primitive stone and turnbuckle guardrails—that is if there are any guardrails at all. At 3,550 feet in elevation, the highway reaches Sitgreaves Pass, where the Summit Station and Ice Cream Parlor stood until 1967. Three states are visible from the summit.

The west side of the grade is not for the faint of heart, plunging 700 feet in 2 miles to Goldroad. The switchbacks can be seen in the 1959 movie *From Here to Eternity*. In the days of gravity-fed carburetors, locals would drive up the hill backwards. In the 1940s, service stations charged $3.50 to tow drivers too timid to tackle the grade.

Route 66 drops to the Gold Road Mine and the ruins of Goldroad. The boomtown sprouted when Jose Jerez discovered gold here in 1900. A government order closed the mines in 1942, and property owners leveled most of the town in 1949 to avoid paying taxes. The Goldroad Mine resumed operations in 1995 but closed in 1998.

Oatman is named for Olive Oatman, held captive for five years by American Indians after her family was massacred. The area population soared to 20,000 before the mines closed. New Route 66 bypassing Oatman opened on September 17, 1952. Within 24 hours, six of the seven gas stations in town had closed. The population fell to about 60.

Oatman now attracts 500,000 tourists annually. The old prospectors turned their burros loose when they were no longer needed. Their descendants now roam the streets freely, cadging carrots and leaving their calling cards on the wooden sidewalks. Colorful shops and cafés line the main street, and shots ring out from staged gunfights.

The Durlin Motel opened in 1902 and later became the Oatman Hotel. Clark Gable and Carol Lombard spent their honeymoon in room 15 on March 29, 1939. A ghost named Oatie, a miner who drank himself to death after his wife and children died, is said to haunt the hotel. Travelers can stay in Gable's or Oatie's rooms. (National Archives.)

In this view at Oatman, Elephant Tooth's Peak looms over the Tom Reed Gold Mine. In 1910, the Vivian Mine was about to close, and Oatman faced hard times. But Ely Hilty, Joe Anderson, and Daniel Tooker discovered this rich vein and launched a second boom. The government closed the mine in 1942, and only ruins remain.

The 1952 Route 66 alignment bypassing Oatman drops south from Kingman through the valley of the Sacramento Wash. At Yucca, establishments like the Joshua Motel and Café quickly sprang up to serve travelers on the new highway. The Joshua and nearly all of those businesses are now in ruins, killed off by Interstate 40.

A traveler's journey across Arizona on Route 66 comes to an end at Topock, Navajo for "many crossings." The community developed in 1883, as construction began on a wooden railroad bridge over the Colorado River. From 1890 until 1914, Joe and Nellie Bush operated the *Nellie T* ferry here. Today nothing remains of these structures.

The jagged peaks in the background gave the town of Needles, California, its name. The Needles were named by Lt. Amiel Weeks Whipple, who led the government railroad survey in 1854. In John Steinbeck's *The Grapes of Wrath*, Tom Joad said, "Never seen such tough mountains. This here's a murder country. This here's the bones of a country."

The steel Red Rock Railroad Bridge opened in 1890. Between 1914 and 1916, planks were laid over the rails and motorists paid a toll to cross between trains. A new railroad span opened in 1945, and the converted Red Rock Bridge began carrying Route 66 on May 21, 1947. Replaced by the Interstate 40 bridge in 1966, it was dismantled in 1976.

The graceful National Old Trails Arch Bridge opened on February 20, 1916. The bridge was featured in the motion picture *The Grapes of Wrath*. It was in danger of being demolished after traffic was shifted to the former railroad bridge but now carries a Pacific Gas and Electric natural gas pipeline across the Colorado River.

Visit us at
arcadiapublishing.com

9 781531 652401

QUEER POWER!

HarperCollins*Publishers*
1 London Bridge Street
London SE1 9GF

www.harpercollins.co.uk

HarperCollins*Publishers*
1st Floor, Watermarque Building,
Ringsend Road, Dublin 4, Ireland

First published by HarperCollins*Publishers* 2021

1 3 5 7 9 10 8 6 4 2

A catalogue record of this book is available
from the British Library

ISBN 978-0-00-843416-8

Printed and bound in Latvia by GPS

MIX
Paper from
responsible sources
FSC™ C007454

This book is produced from independently certified FSC™
paper to ensure responsible forest management.

For more information visit: www.harpercollins.co.uk/green

DOM&INK

QUEER

POWER!

ICONS, ACTIVISTS & GAME CHANGERS FROM ACROSS THE RAINBOW

HarperCollins*Publishers*

CONTENTS

LADY
PHYLL

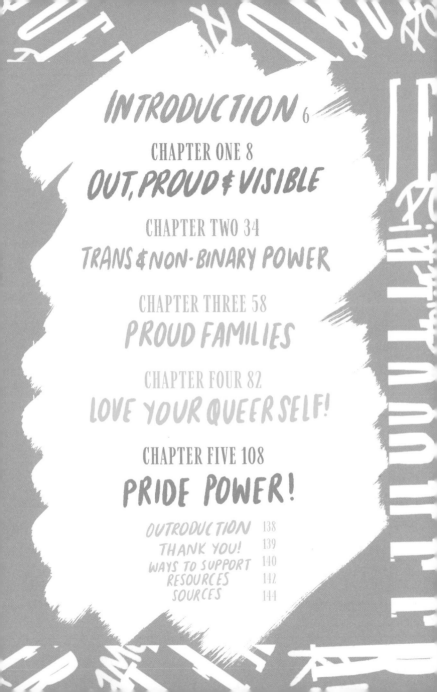

INTRO

When I was growing up, I really struggled to see myself in that many, if any, characters, anywhere. Where was my feminine homo, the lanky-legged queeroe of dreams that I could aspire to be? There were only so many years I could pretend to be Cheetara from *ThunderCats* or Ellie Sattler from *Jurassic Park* (Laura Dern, if you read this, I always look at a pink shirt and cream cargo-short combo and think of you fondly). And here's the thing: I'm a basic bitch white cis gay man. If I struggled in my teen years for representation, I cannot imagine what it must have been, and still be, like for all those who didn't feel seen or represented. That's what drove me to put together *Queer Power*. I wanted to create something for the community, for the allies and for the next generation of queer youth. A book celebrating modern-day trailblazers, activists and icons who have shaped our world and will continue to do so.

I could have gone in a number of different directions. There are a variety of amazing books out there that feature inspiring historical LGBTQ+ figures and I felt they do it so well that I didn't want to take up that space. I really could have pushed more celebrity into *Queer Power* if I wanted to, but I didn't. This book is a mix of hugely well-known public figures and some people you may not recognise. That's the charm. The people in these pages are the ones whose voices should be amplified, whose stories and journeys should be in front of you. These are people that I look up to and am inspired by. People that I have genuinely learnt from. And hope

that you will too. I couldn't fit in everyone I wanted as there are so many incredible humans out there doing the work for the LGBTQ+ community. So once you've finished the book, and re-read it, and lent it to your Aunty Carol, you can get out there and research other voices that need to be heard!

So, no matter where you are on your journey in life, I hope reading about these inspirational icons helps you. This book is a safe space for you, a place to lose yourself in its artwork and remind you to always live your authentically queer truth. I'm here for you.

For me, *Queer Power* isn't just a book full of idols; it's my own love letter to the LGBTQ+ community. I love you.

DOM&INK

PRONOUNS

All pronouns (she/her, he/him, they/them) in this book are the primary pronouns the icon uses.

CHAPTER ONE

OUT, PROUD

AND VISIBLE

It's our first chapter and you're about to meet so many incredible humans. Are you ready, hun? These next few pages are looking at people who are out there and visibly representing not just the LGBTQ+ community but others too. I don't think you can finish reading this without feeling proud of them and what they stand for!

ANICK SONI

@anickians

The intersex community are massively underrepresented and their voices and stories need to be heard. In 2020 alone, there was a huge call to end unnecessary surgery on intersex children without their consent: the Ann & Robert H. Lurie Children's Hospital of Chicago was the first hospital to apologise for performing such surgeries in the past.

Anick Soni is at the forefront of intersex campaigning and activism. His many achievements include receiving the *GAY TIMES* Honour for British Community Trailblazer Award in 2019. Yes, Anick! Having helped to organise UK Black Pride, Pride in London AND the first intersex march, Anick is taking huge steps in advocating for the intersex community.

His visibility and words have been a huge contributor to helping representation and he openly encourages conversations around intersex people, especially in the media. This is mirrored in Anick's FANTASTIC documentary for BBC Radio 1, 'The Intersex Diaries', which charts his own journey to surgery and is powerful, beautiful and informative. I encourage anyone who reads this to watch it straight away. Like, right now, please.

'YOU'VE HEARD THE PHRASE, "I WEAR MY HEART ON MY SLEEVE", WELL, I KINDA WEAR MY PENIS ON MINE'

BLAIR IMANI

@blairimani

Blair Imani is a queer Muslim, historian, author and activist. I think Blair plays a very important part in the queer community and the push for social justice. She came out in June 2017, whilst on Tucker Carlson's Fox News show talking about safe spaces for Muslims in the United States. This was a real turning point and a massive moment of visibility for the Muslim members of the LGBTQ+ community. There is a common misconception that many Muslim people are homophobic. This outdated stereotype completely erases the idea that you can be queer and Muslim, not to mention the experiences of many queer Muslim people who very much exist!

Following the programme, she also wrote a blog post about her coming out and the importance of representation of queer Muslims in mainstream media. This led to an outpouring of messages of support, with many people thankful that they finally felt seen and heard. Reflecting on Instagram, she wrote: 'Sure, since coming out I've been ostracised and lost opportunities but Alhamdulillah being an out and proud Muslim is a blessing that every closeted person of faith deserves to experience.' Blair uses online platforms to further educate her audience on a number of issues surrounding anti-racism, LGBTQ+ and feminism. Her 'Smarter In Seconds' video series is the highlight of my week and I can guarantee after fifteen seconds, you will have learnt not just something, but something *valuable*.

NIKKIE

@nikkietutorials

With over 13.6 million followers on YouTube, *NikkieTutorials*, a.k.a. Nikkie De Jager, is one of the leading trans figures on social media and in the beauty industry. A supremely talented make-up artist, De Jager can serve a fierce face of any kind of glam. In early January 2020, she came out as trans in her video, 'I'm Coming Out', which has had 35 million views and a ton of support, virtual cuddles and love. Coming out for many trans people is a huge thing to do, and this was definitely the case for De Jager. In her video, she revealed she had been blackmailed by someone and came out as a result of not wanting to live in fear. As she said on *The Ellen Show*, 'Plot twist, that didn't happen!'

Whilst it wasn't ideal, coming out in this way took the power away from the blackmailer. Since releasing the video, Nikkie has received unanimous support from celebrities, brands and followers. She now openly speaks on video about her trans journey, each time constantly reminding any trans youth out there that are still afraid, 'As long as I get to be myself and inspire little "Nikkies" to be their selves, that's all I can do.'

DE JAGER

'IF YOU FEEL YOU'RE TRAPPED AND THERE'S NO WAY OUT - KNOW THAT IT GETS BETTER'

LIL NAS X

@lilnasx

Anyone who primarily wears cowboy hats, studded jackets and neon boots so effortlessly, basically is ICONIC in my eyes. In August 2019, 'Old Town Road', a country rap song, sat atop the Billboard 100 for nineteen weeks, the longest any single had stayed at number one since the chart began in 1958. Furthermore, Nas came out as gay whilst the single was dominating the charts at number one, therefore making him the only person to do so at the same time as having a number-one record. Historic.

After coming out, Nas revealed on Twitter that he thought he'd made it obvious with his rainbow-themed album cover and the lyrics on his track 'C7osure'. Whilst he received a homophobic backlash from parts of the hip-hop community, Nas also had a lot of amazing support, with many fans who were Black and queer pointing out how inspiring it was to see a Black queer man succeeding in mainstream music.

Since coming out, Nas has released more top hits, modelled for Rihanna's Fenty Beauty, won awards and was named by *TIME* magazine as one of 'the 25 most influential people on the Internet'. He also still wears his signature looks, which incorporate queerness with camp humour, some futuristic aspects and a whole lot of attitude.

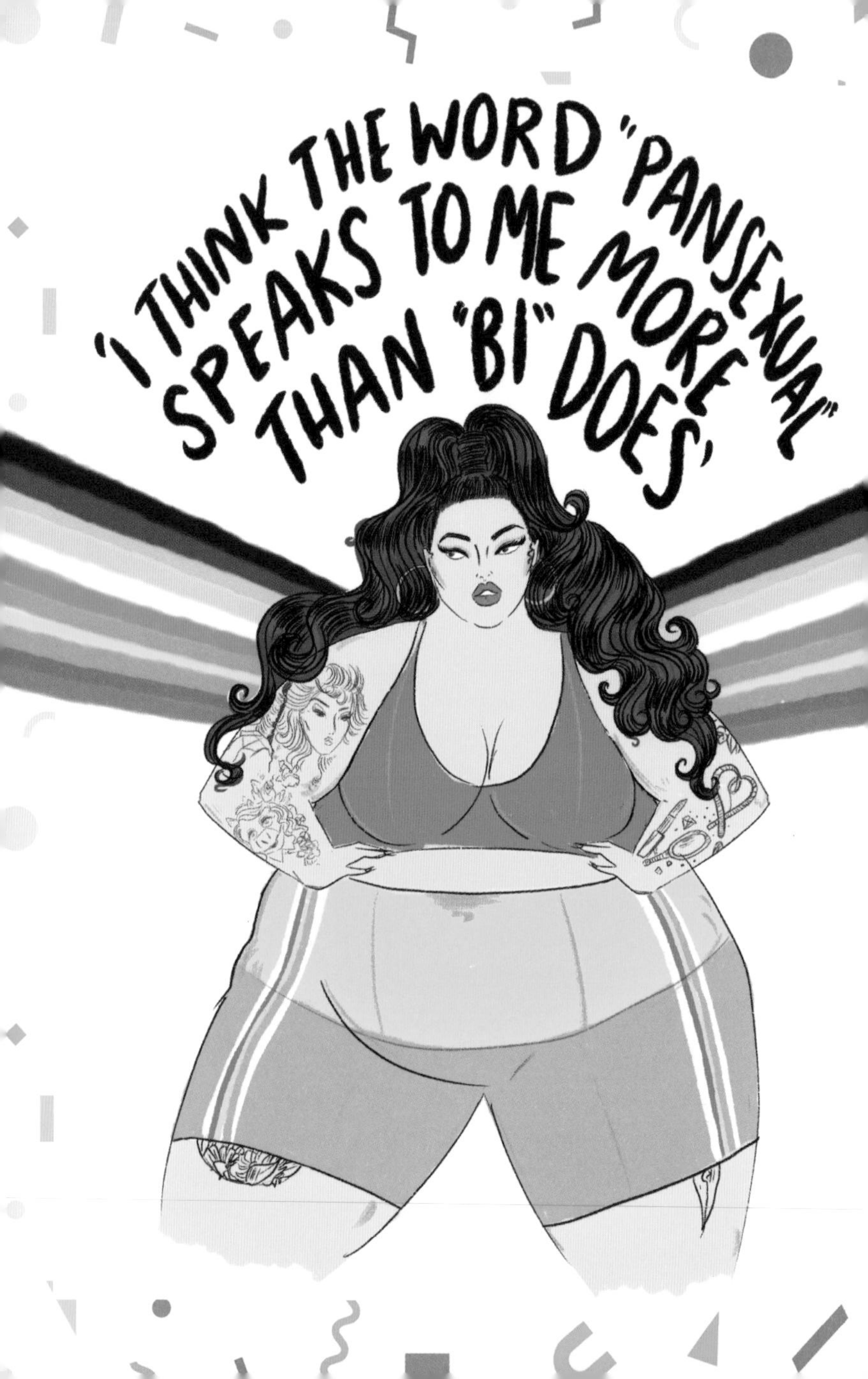
"I THINK THE WORD "PANSEXUAL" SPEAKS TO ME MORE THAN "BI" DOES."

TESS HOLLIDAY

@tessholliday

In 2013, Tess started her #effyourbeautystandards movement on Instagram, which is all about promoting body positivity, inclusivity and, importantly, the idea that you DON'T have to be a certain size to love your body. YAS. She launched her latest fashion range based around the movement in August 2020, in collaboration with Fashion To Figure, and I am in awe of how beautifully diverse it is. She had plus-size models who were Black, trans and disabled. Yes, inclusivity. We love to see it.

Aside from gracing the covers of magazines, being a model and an author, Tess is also very passionate about her activism. She constantly speaks up about LGBTQ+ rights, racism, ableism and more on her social media and uses her platform to raise so much awareness for these key issues. Her raw honesty and direct approach are what make people love her (me included, times a million).

Speaking in 2019 about coming out as pansexual, she said, 'I can connect with people on a more intimate level than I was before, because I don't have to pretend to be someone I'm not.'

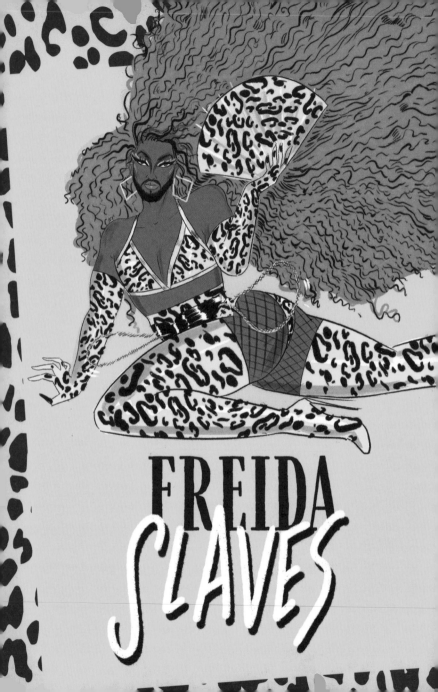

FREIDA
SLAVES

@freidaslaves

East London queen Freida Slaves is a fierce force to be reckoned with. I actually had the absolute pleasure of seeing Freida perform last year and, OH MY CHER, she was incredible. Inspired by Janet Jackson, Beyoncé, Paula Abdul and Madonna, Freida exudes fierceness and she KNOWS how to control a room. She was also a professional dancer, so you know that choreo is nailed tight.

Drag performers are a huge part of the LGBTQ+ community. Their performances and appearances are not always just about lip sync but also touch on raising awareness of key issues and how we as a community can unite against them. Freida is no exception. Any time she is interviewed she always uses the opportunity to speak up about the lack of representation of Black drag queens and drag queens of colour and how her visibility speaks so much to the marginalised members of our rainbow family.

Speaking to *HISKIND*, she said, '. . . the more I spread the word and showcase myself, the more queens of colour will emerge.' This is so important, and it's really crucial that we all continue to support and uplift these voices so they can keep creating and entertaining us with their talents.

'YOU SEE A BLACK DRAG QUEEN, JUST LIVING HER BEST LIFE'

'NORMALISE DISABLED BODIES. NORMALISE TRANS BODIES. NORMALISE PEOPLE LOOKING HOWEVER THE F#⧵K THEY WANT'

@thedisabledhippie

'People are always so hyper-focused on how a disabled person or a trans person is supposed to look or act. I'm gonna need you to throw that idea in the trash,' writes Julian Gavino on a post on his Instagram, with him sat in his wheelchair, eyes closed, a soft red cardigan draped over his arms, ripped striped jeans covering his legs, as his long locks of hair sit on his shoulders. Deconstructing prejudices on how disabled and trans people are viewed and also serving a look? WERK.

Hailing from Florida, Julian Gavino is a trans-masc, disabled, awesome human who is an activist, writer, life coach and model. He was born with Ehlers-Danlos syndrome, which affects the connective tissues in his body. Whilst also navigating life as trans, Julian makes sure he uses his platform and the work he gets with brands to write and speak about the importance of trans AND disabled bodies. Through his activism, he has spoken about how important it is for intersectional queer people to be recognised: 'At the end of the day, it doesn't matter if there are 10 million LGBTQIA+ disabled folx or five in the entire world. Those people still need representation.'

ALEXANDER LEON

@alexand_erleon

Alexander Leon is a writer, campaigner and activist. His work centres on diversity, inclusion, LGBTQ+ rights, anti-racism and mental health. He also has the most adorable Australian accent ever – warm, comforting and like an audio hug. Alexander consistently tweets and posts about racism within the LGBTQ+ community and how we can identify it and challenge it.

His post, 'Why Is Racism A Queer Issue', highlights this in the opening slide: 'White LGBTQ+ people have a responsibility to understand the effect of anti-blackness and other forms of racism in our community.' This is further highlighted by the small backlash Alexander has to deal with whenever he posts something like this – we have so much more work to do as a community to actively be anti-racist. I would also suggest checking out Alexander's Twitter, as his tweets are SO on point. He manages to deconstruct hypermasculinity and performative masculinity, and speaks to me on so many emotional levels in 250 characters or less in the space of three minutes. There's a power in that.

'JUST BECAUSE THE WORLD IS STILL CATCHING UP TO OUR GREATNESS, DOESN'T MEAN YOU WEREN'T ALWAYS GREAT'

RINA SAWAYAMA

@rinasonline

A Japanese-British singer-songwriter, Rina Sawayama is the pansexual queer pop icon the world needs right now. Her debut album, *Sawayama*, is packed full of songs about self-expression and sexuality, and is a full-on queertastic experience in every way. Previously identifying as bisexual, Rina came out as pansexual in 2018 in *Vice* magazine: 'For me there's still a lack of representation. I just think the reason I wasn't so comfortable with my sexuality was because there was no one on TV or anywhere that I could point to and go, "Look, Mom! This person is what I was talking about!"'

Rina used this moment to discuss the deeper themes of her lyrics, past experiences and her identity. She was also fully aware of how people would view her, as she was in a heterosexual relationship at the time. Her song 'Cherry' touches on this viewpoint, that bi and pan people 'don't feel authentically queer when they're in heterosexual relationships'. I think it's really important to say here that no matter where you are on your queer journey, or who you're with, *every* part of you deserves and should be accepted by a queer safe space. Always. On that note, go stream 'Cherry' now.

ARUN BLAIR-MANGAT

@arunblair

Arun Blair-Mangat, or A.B.M., as I like to call him, is an incredible gender queer actor, composer and talented singer of notes no-human-can-ever-reach, especially me (I have tried numerous times).

In 2019, he starred in *& Juliet*, a revisionist musical based on the story of Shakespeare's *Romeo and Juliet*. His character is the non-binary character, May, one of the many large supporting characters in the ensemble piece. May's journey is central to the story of *& Juliet*. What I love about A.B.M. is how he has worked so hard to make sure he represents the non-binary community correctly and sensitively. When I went to see the show, it was the first time I'd seen a gender non-conforming main character in a West End musical. A.B.M. has a talent for holding the audience captive whilst educating them at the same time.

As he said to *Attitude* magazine in February 2020, 'This is the most that I've loved myself in a long time because I'm so satiated by this show.'

'IT ALLOWS ME TO EMBRACE MY OTHERNESS; IT CELEBRATES THAT'

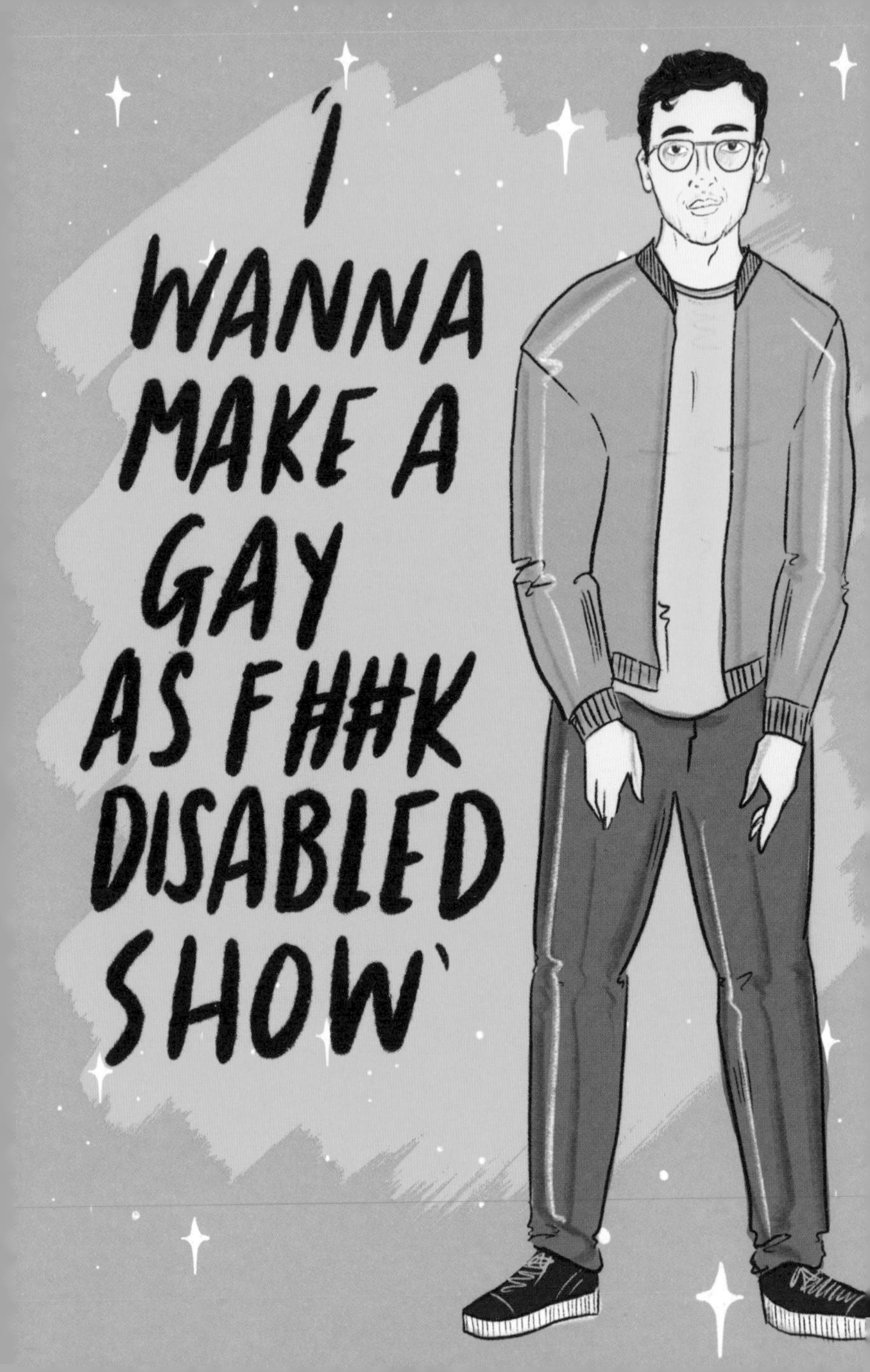
'I WANNA MAKE A GAY AS F##K DISABLED SHOW'

RYAN O'CONNELL

@ryanoconn

I remember sitting down to watch *Special* on Netflix and then spending the following three hours feeling a multitude of emotions. It's funny, it's sad, it's progressive AF. It's just amazing. So, if you haven't watched it yet, I advise you do. The show relates to viewers on multiple levels, whilst also incorporating themes of body positivity, mental health, queer rights and ableism too.

The lead character is played by Ryan O'Connell, the writer and creator of the series. It's a semi-autobiographical take on O'Connell's own life story – navigating being queer and having cerebral palsy whilst living in LA. Originally, O'Connell didn't think *Special* would happen. Speaking to *Deadline* he said, 'It was really, really hard to sell a show with a gay, disabled lead, quite frankly, so we had to take a lot of different pathways to getting it made.' *Special* is now an Emmy-nominated show, which is a massive achievement, especially in the movement for representation of the disabled community in the media. The LGBTQ+ community is so vast and varied, and shows like *Special* are so important in order that every part of the rainbow feels valid and visible.

THINGS TO CONSIDER WHEN COMING OUT:

Firstly, only come out when YOU are ready. No one should ever tell you how or when to come out; that's something that only you will know. If you don't feel the timing is right, then don't do it – that's okay! When you do decide that the time is right, here are some tips to help you slam those closet doors wide open. If you've done this already or you're not queer, share these tips with people in your life who might need them.

1. YOU DON'T NEED TO LABEL YOURSELF

Whatever stage you're at in your journey, you really don't need to label yourself. Some people come out as gay, then through experiences and life, realise they're bisexual or pan, or whatever they want to identify as sexually. 'Queer' is an inclusive term that can be used for a number of sexualities. Don't feel pressured to label yourself, there's only one YOU and that's what makes you so unique.

2. GENDER ROLES

So – and this could do with a whole book in itself – please leave those preconceived ideas of gender tucked away somewhere. You just need to forget the ideas that the woman in the relationship does this and the man does that. The beauty of the queer community is that there are so many different variations of relationships and what you want for yours doesn't need to be set around very old views of gender. Keep an open mind and embrace anything.

3. LEARN SOME SHIT

The LGBTQ+ community has a history of queer rights, fights for equality and important figures. Read up on some icons who paved the way. Learning LGBTQ+ history is a privilege. It will remind you how far we have come and the struggles we've faced. LGBTQ+ rights are not equal everywhere, so consider this when thinking about how you can support others.

4. CONFIDE IN SOMEONE

Telling a friend first and actually vocalising how you feel is a great step forward in coming out to others. I remember telling a friend and the burden immediately felt a little less heavy. Make sure it's someone who knows you and that you can trust them with your little queer heart. If you're really conscious about telling a friend, I'd suggest talking to someone on a queer helpline first. Take your time and take it steady. Don't rush yourself.

5. WERK THAT COMMITTEE

If you're coming out and this affects your work, I'd suggest enquiring about whether there is an LGBTQ+ committee. Most workplaces should have something like this, so maybe reach out to them and ask about their experiences being queer in the workplace. Also, new queer friends. YAY.

6. SOCIAL AND SAFE

On your social media, follow, share and repost queer creators. You don't have to make your whole feed rainbowlicious, but following a few LGBTQ+ accounts you can personally relate to or feel seen by is a great reminder that you are valid, loved and there are people out there doing their thing, and you can TOO. Curate your social media to be an online safe space. If you don't follow me I won't be offended . . . *goes and cries in gay listening to Sinead O' Connor*.

CHAPTER TWO

TRANS-NON-& NON BINARY POWER!

The trans and non-binary community make up a hugely important part of the LGBTQ+ family. Unfortunately, not everywhere in the world sees it that way and the 'T' of the LGBTQ+ needs more support and love than ever. The following are icons who are out there, actively pushing for more trans representation and fighting for their rights and for justice at the same time.

DOMINIQUE JACKSON

@dominique.a.r.jackson

Tobagonian-American actress, model and real-life ballroom queen, Dominique Jackson is known to most for her role of Elektra on television's *Pose*. If you haven't seen it yet, where have you been, hun? An original ballroom legend herself, Dominique cemented her status in the House of Sinclair in NYC. She pursued different modelling gigs and acting opportunities and eventually landed a role in *Pose*, a show set in the late 1980s that focuses on the ballroom scene. The show made history for having the largest cast of transgender actors playing transgender characters.

Having since become a pop culture and queer icon, Dominique has also used her voice for the trans community, openly talking about her experiences growing up and working with many different LGBTQ+ charities and organisations. Her passionate speech at the Human Rights Campaign's National Dinner in 2019 is really powerful and a must-watch.

CHELLA MAN

@chellaman

Having documented his transition on YouTube to more than 4 million viewers, Chella Man is the deaf, Chinese and Jewish activist the world needs right now. Chella uses his continually growing space on YouTube for open conversation around his relationships, art, activism and more. At just 21 years old, he has been a TEDx speaker, modelled for Calvin Klein and starred as a DC superhero in *Titans*. He uses his YouTube videos and Instagram posts to speak up for the LGBTQ+ disabled community and advocate for their need to have their voices heard and seen.

Chella Man is also the FIRST trans-masculine and deaf person to sign with IMG Models. Working as a model and actor, he also pushes for better visibility for disabled queer performers. Speaking to *Vogue*, he quite rightly said, 'Overall, until disabled, queer BIPoC representation mirrors how the world is as it is, true inclusivity is yet to be reached.' Chella also documents and shares his relationship with his partner, MaryV Benoit. It's beautiful and adorable and so needed. We need to see more queer love!

KENNY
ETHAN
JONES

@kennyethanjones

Kenny Ethan Jones is a transgender model and activist and all-round awesome human. What I think makes Kenny really important is that he openly speaks up and talks about trans and gender non-conforming people who menstruate.

I hadn't really seen this topic covered outside cis bodies much (well, ever) until I FOUND Kenny. He gained attention in 2018 as the first transgender man to front a UK period campaign from Pink Parcel. This was a huge turning point and made history. The fact that Kenny was even in that campaign will have helped, and will continue to help, so that many trans and gender non-conforming people have someone to relate to and represent them. Since then, Kenny has been on the cover of magazines and he talks frequently about body politics, mental health and intimacy. One of my favourite quotes of his is this:
'You don't have to be the toxic masculinity of manhood to be valid as a man.'

JUNO DAWSON

@junodawson

Juno Dawson is a trans author and actress from Yorkshire. To date, she has written around twenty books and is basically a book machine (I'm not complaining – every book she has authored is fantastic and carries an important message for the reader!). She is also often found taking part in different trans rights marches – she puts it best herself on her Instagram: 'So once again, I am spending a Saturday screaming at Parliament because it feels like the right thing to do.'

We're living in a time where trans rights are frequently under attack and it's crucial we have figures like Juno taking up space and talking about their experiences. It's also imperative that we keep supporting trans writers and their books. Juno's work, and Juno herself, speaks to and relates to so many trans and queer people out there. And she does it all so well in a sequin blazer, too. Her latest young adult book, *Wonderland*, features a trans lead character, which proves you can have a bestselling book for teens without needing a boy wizard. So far, the book has been a bestseller, had numerous rave reviews and been featured as part of the Zoella Book Club. All whilst during a pandemic. I bow to you Queen Juno!

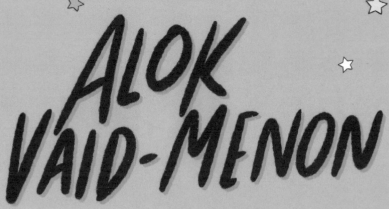

ALOK VAID-MENON

@alokvmenon

Alok is an Indian-American, trans feminine writer and activist. Texas-born and based in New York, they have become a staple in the online LGBTQ+ community for their extensive work around equality for gender non-conforming people. All of Alok's captions carry a resonance and weight. Throughout 2020, they were vocal about Black Lives Matter, speaking on Black Trans Lives and all the work we still have to do to challenge racism and transphobia.

Alok also consistently keeps the conversation going around gender. In a world where more and more people identify as non-binary, Alok continues to use their platform to give this community a voice. They encourage their audience to embrace all ideas of gender and what gender is. 'One gender, one aesthetic, one medium, one field . . . Things are so much more fluid than that. I fundamentally believe in cross-pollination,' they told *GQ*.

'I HAVE FOUND BEAUTY IN SO MANY PLACES WHERE I WAS TAUGHT SHAME, MY FRIENDSHIPS ARE DEEP & VULNERABLE, I KNOW FIRMLY & IRREVOCABLY WHO I AM'

RADAM RIDWAN

@radamridwan

Lots of people created social media side-hustles during the 2020 lockdown. Radam Ridwan was no exception. Radam created the online #lockdownlookbook where they posted a full fashion look to their Instagram grid every single day, for the whole of lockdown. I'm talking platform boots, tassels, sequins, bits of nudity. EVERYTHING. They also have an amazing collection of hats. Looks like these made my day – and a whole lot of other people's – a lot more glamorous. Radam interspersed these posts with thoughtfully written words on fighting transphobia, ultimately creating different calls to action on how to support the gender non-conforming and trans community.

Whilst Radam knows how to serve a look, their words on their experiences of how they are treated day-to-day are a sombre reminder that we need to keep supporting and protecting our non-binary folk against threats. We have to keep on raising their voices online and offline so that they can be heard.

'THE BIG PROBLEM FOR NON-BINARY PEOPLE LIKE ME ISN'T JUST BEING SEEN – IT'S BEING SEEN AS HUMAN'

INDYA MOORE

@indyamoore

Named one of *TIME* magazine's 100 Most Influential People in 2019, Indya Moore is a transgender non-binary force of awesomeness. Indya left home at fourteen and grew up in foster care. They worked as a sex worker and went through drug addiction, homelessness and hormone treatment. They managed to overcome these experiences and channel them into their role as Angel on *Pose*. The show became a huge success and Indya became an overnight name, one of the most prominent faces for a transgender non-binary person of colour on television and in the public eye.

Since then, Indya has modelled for Calvin Klein and Louis Vuitton, and made their runway debut at New York Fashion Week 2020 for Jason Wu. Indya always takes the opportunity to speak about their activism work around trans rights. Speaking to the E! channel on the red carpet at the 2019 Emmys, Indya was vocal about the importance of trans people in fashion spaces, such as their own work as an ambassador for Louis Vuitton. They said, 'It's more tricky to exist than to walk in this dress.'

DANIELA VEGA

@dani.vega.h

Daniela Vega is a Chilean actress mostly known for her career-defining, award-winning role in *A Fantastic Woman*. She was the FIRST transgender person in history to present an award at the Academy Awards ceremony, in 2018. Taking to the stage, ruffles galore and elegance personified in a pink fuchsia gown by Maria Lucia Hohan, she addressed the crowd, asking them to 'open their hearts'. *TIME* magazine coined the moment by naming Daniela the 'Breakout Oscars Star' of that year.

A Fantastic Woman won the Oscar for Best Foreign Language Film and drew international attention to Daniela. This was a turning point for transgender rights in Chile and helped push forward a bill (from 2013) for trans people to legally change their names and gender on official documents. This bill eventually took effect in 2019 with Daniela reflecting on her Instagram and sharing a message of support: 'I dedicate this day to the beautiful conquest of ruling the name.'

CHARLIE
CRAGGS

@charlie_craggs

Founder of Nail Transphobia, author and self-proclaimed 'bad bitch', Charlie Craggs runs pop-up nail salons across the UK, where she and her team of trans and non-binary nail technicians are there to buff, polish and educate you on trans rights and activism, whilst also serving you some nailtastic art to serve and slay with.

In 2017, she released her book *To My Trans Sisters* – an anthology of 100 letters by trans women, about and FOR trans women. The book was nominated for a number of awards and was also a finalist in the 30th Lambda Literary Awards.

Described as the 'Voice of a community' by *Vogue* (OMG! right?), Charlie Craggs is never afraid to speak her mind and call out brands, public figures and others on transphobia. What I love about Charlie is that she is always authentically herself and does not and will not change for anyone. She openly talks about her surgeries, dating, sex and more on social media, and I myself have learnt SO much from her.

In 2018, Charlie was part of a campaign for inclusion of a transgender rainbow flag in Unicode, which, as of the time of writing, is about to be included in 2020. YES, CHARLIE. TRANS RIGHTS!

CRYSTAL
RASMUSSEN

@tomglitter

Crystal Rasmussen is a non-binary drag performer, author, writer and an absolute ICON in London. They combine a sharp wit, the vocal range of Mariah Carey and the thigh-high snakeskin boots of my dreams. A multi-talented performer, Crystal took their one-queen show, *The Bible 2,* to Edinburgh Fringe and London and received rave reviews. They also host *Dragony Aunts* for Comedy Central. On top of that, Crystal also wrote the brilliantly funny *Diary of a Drag Queen*, their semi-autobiographical book on their own queer experiences that take place over a year. Basically, Crystal can do anything and everything.

When I first met Crystal I was taken in by how glamorous they were, how funny they were, but also how kind they were. There's something in Crystal's big blue eyes that just makes you feel at home and loved. Magical humans like Crystal are very hard to come by in this world and they always promote a message of inclusivity and self-love.

'UR POWER RADIATES AND UR FLUIDITY IN WHATEVER FORM IS NOT ONLY VALID, IT'S BEAUTIFUL'

HOW TO BE AN ALLY TO THE TRANS & NON-BINARY COMMUNITY:

As a cis white queer man, I have no space to talk about what it's like to transition or come out as trans or gender non-conforming. However, I can help you become an ally to the trans community, which is especially vulnerable right now. If you're reading this and aren't cis, and you think it would help, please show these pages to loved ones. Maybe take a pic or lend the book, share with friends and spread the word of trans allyship! Yes!

1. DONATE

There are trans funds/mutual aids and charities you can support with as little as a fiver. That money goes a long way. You could do a one-off payment or even set up a standing order. If that's not financially viable, perhaps share the link on your socials so other people who can afford to can help out. Better yet, organise a fundraiser! There are people transitioning, needing surgeries or therapy across the world 24/7, so anything you can do to help them get closer to what they need is amazing.

2. SIGN AND SHARE

There are petitions all over social media relating to government bills, fighting for equality for trans people and justice for the families of trans people who have been killed. These are important to show those in power the outrage at what is going on. With enough signatures, we can get justice! Stick a link in your bio, start a WhatsApp chain – keep sharing.

3. SUPPORT TRANS AND NON-BINARY CREATORS

Social media is FULL of trans and non-binary creators, authors, actors, singers and more. However, not all big brands will approach them and involve them with work outside of Pride season. Follow them, like them, share their work with your followers. These people need to be seen and their stories need to be heard. Go watch their YouTube videos, buy their T-shirts and read their books. Whatever you do will go directly towards helping them and letting them know they have support out there.

4. TALK IT OUT

There may be situations where a friend, a family member, or in my case once, a date, is being 'problematic' in their views on trans people. These are moments for this person to learn and grow, so have a conversation with them about what they've said and how that affects the larger community. I've had awkward conversations with people where I've pulled them up on something and a year later I've seen them pull someone else up on their words around trans and non-binary people. More of this, please.

5. SUPPORT TRANS AUTHORS

Read trans authors! Read books with trans characters! The publishing industry needs more representation in terms of trans writing and the best way to let them know is by buying their books, tweeting how much you love them and supporting the authors.

6. START LEARNING

There are numerous lists on the Internet for learning more about the history of trans and non-binary people. There are books, films, documentaries, podcasts, songs and more! Shows like *Pose* are gateways for cis people to learn and see what has to be done going forward. Don't stop at one show; consume as much information as you can.

CHAPTER THREE

PROUD FAMILIES

These are icons that come from a wide range of different families – a family doesn't always need to be blood related. As queer people, we have a lot to navigate with our family; sometimes it's good, sometimes not so good. With that, there is a special power in discovering your 'chosen' family! This chapter also touches on allies for the queer community and what they've done to help fight for LGBTQ+ rights.

SABAH

CHOUDREY

@sabah.c

In Sabah Choudrey's own words, they're a 'reluctant activist on most things trans, brown and hairy'. Speaker, writer and performer, Sabah is also the Head of Youth Services at Gendered Intelligence and co-founder of Colours Youth UK, an organisation that helps Black and PoC queer youth navigate their experiences through workshops, mentoring schemes and more. Safe spaces like these are essential for those who are marginalised within the LGBTQ+ community, to remind them they have a chosen family and also to celebrate who they are and how far they have come.

As a trans youth worker for Gendered Intelligence, Sabah has been vocal about trans rights and how important it is we keep fighting for the trans youth of tomorrow. They provide downloadable resources and content on their website so anyone can educate themselves on how to support and be an ally. What a legend.

THE WORK WE DO ON OURSELVES IS AS IMPORTANT AS THE WORK WE DO FOR OUR YOUNG PEOPLE

THE UNION/ WADE FAMILY

@zayawade

Daughter of actress Gabrielle Union and retired NBA star Dwyane Wade, thirteen-year-old Zaya Wade came out as trans in early 2020. Both parents publicly spoke out so well about their daughter's experience, they are a shining example of how to act when someone you love comes out as trans. Dwyane even went as far as designing some custom Pride trainers for his daughter.

'We're just trying to figure out as much information as we can to make sure that we give our child the best opportunity to be, you know, her best self,' Dwyane said on *The Ellen Show*. Since then, Zaya has become an emerging figure of trans youth and had her red-carpet debut at The Truth Awards with her parents, the trio wearing a full coordinated matching ensemble. Now *that* is how you do trans allyship as parents.

'YOU ARE A LEADER. IT'S OUR OPPORTUNITY TO ALLOW YOU TO BE A VOICE' DWYANE WADE

'I'M JUST CONSTANTLY TRYING TO LEARN AND NOT SPEAK FOR OTHER PEOPLE, BUT SPEAK WITH THEM. THAT'S A BIG PART OF MY ALLY JOURNEY'

JADE THIRLWALL

@jadethirlwall

Jade Thirlwall is a member of internationally acclaimed girl group Little Mix. Not only is she a total queen, she is also a fantastic ally to the LGBTQ+ community. Using her platform and through her role as a Stonewall UK ambassador, she consistently speaks up for queer rights and trans rights, taking part in marches, protests and sharing valuable information with her followers. With such an engaged following, Jade is showing her audience HOW to be an ally and help raise LGBTQ+ voices up and support these movements in an authentic way.

In an interview with *Attitude*, she said, 'I've really tried to find ways of, like I've said before, walking the walk instead of just talking the talk, and really trying to show them that I'm doing all that I can to help.' I for one truly value the honest and passionate work Jade does for the community by speaking up for us *and* showing up. She also serves a fierce leotard and fan combo lewk, am I right? Now, go stream some Little Mix in your kitchen, please.

65

TE TE BANG

@tete_bang

TeTe Bang is a DJ and female drag performer and the star of Channel 4's drag makeover show, *Drag SOS*. As a female drag queen, TeTe has her existence and drag artistry questioned just because of her gender. This really shouldn't be happening these days, but some people need a reminder – so, in case you're reading this and thinking that, just check yourself, hun, because drag is art and drag is for EVERYONE, not just cis men.

Every look TeTe creates is a playful eleganza of colour, camp and pink and she designs and makes a lot of them herself. During lockdown, she even created 'TeTe's Tutorials', short draggy D.I.Y. videos on how to add volume to wigs, create headdresses, sew dresses and more! Excuse me, whilst I go and attempt to make a custom gogo dress with matching headdress . . .

'I WAS FORTUNATE ENOUGH TO BE BROUGHT UP AROUND STRONG WOMEN WHO TAUGHT ME TO BE BOLD AND EXPRESS HOW I FEEL'

LADY GAGA

@ladygaga

She's Mother Monster. She's Queen of Chromatica. She's a total queer symbol of joy and hope and is solely responsible for shoulder pads and peplums making a comeback in 2008. She's Lady Gaga! Musician, writer, actress and many other things, Gaga has been a solid supporter of the LGBTQ+ community throughout her many years of stardom.

Here's a brief overview – she organised her fans to help volunteer in supporting queer homeless youth at shelters across the US, she continually fights for her LGBTQ+ fans in countries where they have no rights, such as Russia, she's spoken up about homophobia in the music industry, spoken at Stonewall rallies and delivered us the queertastically empowering anthem, 'Born This Way'. For me, the most important moment was when, in 2011, asked in an interview 'if she had a penis', instead of denying it, she said, 'Maybe I do. Would it be so terrible?'

'THIS COMMUNITY HAS FOUGHT AND CONTINUED TO FIGHT A WAR OF ACCEPTANCE, A WAR OF TOLERANCE, AND THE MOST RELENTLESS *BRAVERY*'

TANYA COMPAS

@tanyacompas

Tanya Compas is a freelance youth worker and engagement specialist. During the pandemic and at the height of the Black Lives Matter movement, Tanya founded the brilliant Exist Loudly Fund. In setting up a GoFundMe page, Tanya wanted to create a way to raise money for her workshops for Black queer youth to help them find that safe space in their lives. She also wanted to create a space where they could meet others they can relate to and form relationships with.

The GoFundMe page went viral and Tanya was featured in *Vogue* and *GAY TIMES*. Through Tanya's constant hard work and passion, she managed to raise over £100,392! Yes! Tanya shared the extra finances among other queer funds and organisations. She is a truly inspirational person for so many, especially for all the work she does with the Black and PoC queer community. These spaces are so needed right now. As she wrote on Instagram when she shared the news: 'I am so happy to be able to use my social media platform to create tangible change in our communities to help queer & trans Black and PoC youth.'

PABLLO VITTAR

@pabllovittar

In Brazil, LGBTQ+ rights are still under attack and homophobia even now isn't considered a crime. The country has 300 active organisations working towards equal rights and figures like drag queen and pop star Pabllo Vittar are so important to the movement. In 2014, after going viral singing on local TV in Brazil, Pabllo's career began to take off. Fast forward to 2020 and she has over 10 million followers on Instagram, has graced the cover of many magazines and performed at the MTV European Music Awards.

Pabllo's visibility and her message of equality have been an integral part of many interviews. She refuses to hide who she is and wants to be seen so that the queer youth in Brazil growing up have someone to look up to and aspire to. Her existence in itself is a rebellion against the Brazilian government's views towards the LGBTQ+ community. She herself said in an interview with *Vogue*, 'This is what makes my job worth it, to change other people's lives, or it wouldn't be worth it.'

DRAG
Syndrome

@dragsyndrome

Gaia Callas, Lady Francesca, Horrora Shebang and Justin Bond make up Drag Syndrome, the world's first collective of drag performers with Down's syndrome, who are out there to challenge stereotypes and create a stage for people with learning disabilities. Founder and artistic director Daniel Vais runs a dance company called Culture Device that works with dancers with Down's syndrome. Eventually, some of his performers expressed an interest in wanting to perform in drag. Daniel booked their first gig, something he intended to be a one-off. The gig sold out and the rest is history.

As their popularity grew, Drag Syndrome have been featured in British *Vogue* and performed at DragCon UK. Queer spaces aren't always the most accessible for disabled members of the community, so a group like Drag Syndrome are a welcome step forward in progress for representation and more inclusivity for the queer disabled community.

'ART IS VERY POWERFUL, AND ART AND CULTURE IS VERY IMPORTANT. PEOPLE WITH DOWN'S SYNDROME BRING THE HEART TO THE ART'
FOUNDER, DANIEL VAIS

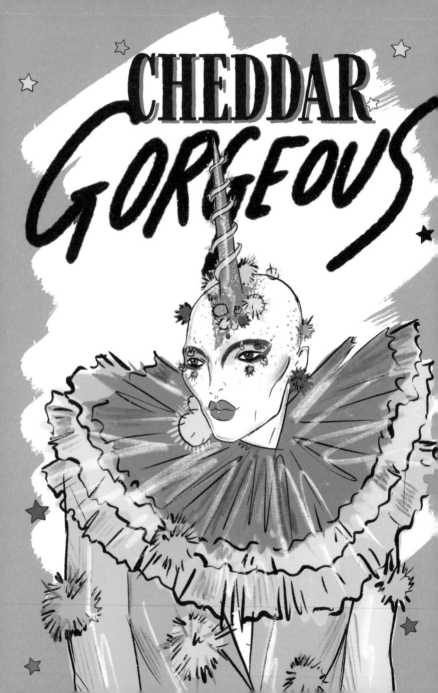

@cheddar_gorgeous

It's not every day you come across a drag unicorn, but then that's what makes Cheddar Gorgeous so great. Cheddar is also a star on Channel 4's drag makeover show, *Drag SOS* (highly recommended viewing, huns) and – plot twist ahoy – an academic who knows a whole lot of stuff about anthropology. Cheddar is at the beating heart of the Manchester LGBTQ+ community AND with their drag family, the Family Gorgeous.

With brains, sequins and a unicorn horn, Cheddar also frequently speaks up about current issues and how we as a community can face them. At their TEDx talk (yup, Cheddar is a TEDx speaker TOO), 'The Power of Drag', they said something about drag and identity that really stuck with me: 'I believe that drag is one of the most powerful forms of self-exploration, expression and political action.'

> WHETHER YOU'RE MALE, FEMALE, STRAIGHT OR GAY, OLD OR YOUNG, DRAG IS ALL ABOUT FINDING YOUR INNER MOST GLAMOROUS ROUTE TO SELF-CONFIDENCE

JESSIE WARE

@jessieware

It's not every day you get an ally pop-star queen who dedicates an album as a 'thank you' to the LGBTQ+ community. However, Jessie Ware did just that. In 2020, during Pride month and with the Black Lives Matter movement on the rise, Jessie released *What's Your Pleasure*, an incredible disco-infused album of power, sensuality and tunes that make your hips wiggle. Speaking with *GAY TIMES*, she mentioned how her queer fans had embraced her music over the years and how her latest offering is a 'safe space where we can dance, feel free and express yourself'. She uses her huge platform to speak out about LGBTQ+ rights and remind her fans that along with her music, she is also a safe space for the community, and will continually support and be an ally to them.

Jessie released two videos for the single, also entitled 'What's Your Pleasure', one a dance video featuring the incredible Black queer dancer, Nicolas Huchard, in a variety of wigs, heels and outfits (honestly, you have to watch it). The second featured Jessie serving a ton of looks herself, including this uber-camp leather dress with the most over-the-top hair I have ever seen (styled by hair king Patrick Wilson). As Dolly Parton once said, 'The higher the hair, the closer to God' – I truly believe this hair reached past God, past the universe and now lives in its own queertastic dimension of awesomeness surrounded by rainbows and looks down on us with love and pride.

ALLY
Alert

HOW TO BE A SUPPORT TO A QUEER PERSON:

You may not feel like this title applies to you but it does. Queer people have varying experiences of trauma, pain and rejection and they carry those feelings with them as they navigate life. Sure, this page is for your cis straight friends, but maybe this page is also a reminder for you on how to check in with your queer chosen family, or even yourself?

1. LISTEN

Listening is a powerful way to get to know someone. *Offering* to listen is even more powerful, as you're literally saying to someone, 'You can be vulnerable with me and I'm a safe space.' Sometimes a person just needs to RANT – I get that – and for you, it may feel like a lot to listen, but to the person offloading their pain, anxieties and whatever else, that will really mean so much to them.

2. CHECK IN ON THEM

Whether someone is going through something in your group or not, I always think it's good to check in on them. If I haven't heard from someone in a few days I'll even message them sometimes saying, 'Just checking in, how you doing?' (Normally followed by a dinosaur emoji.) In some instances I'll get a reply that they're 'fine', just 'super busy' and in other instances they'll start to open up. The feeling that someone is thinking of you and wants to know you're okay is really quite something, so let your friends know.

3. GO TO QUEER SPACES

The amount of times growing up I had people tell me they wouldn't go to a bar because it was 'gay' is off the charts. A great way to support a queer person is going to a queer pub or show or drag night with them; it shows you want to support them and be part of their world. Also, it's guaranteed to be the BEST TIME. If you're not LGBTQ+, be aware you're taking up room in a queer space and respect that. You're always welcome in those spaces, just be aware that they exist to help queer people feel safe and are somewhere they can fully be every colour of the rainbow they want to be.

4. AVOID SAYING MICRO-AGGRESSIONS

Have a read about things to say and not say to a queer person. People sometimes say shit that really isn't cool. When I worked in retail (for a long time), I had a lot thrown at me. Micro-aggressions like 'You don't look gay' or 'Who's the man and who's the woman' just aren't fun, and not all queer people feel comfortable answering them, so if you do say one, be sure to call yourself out, and if someone else says something, call them out, hun!

5. LET THEM KNOW YOU'RE A SAFE SPACE

It's always good in the home, workplace or wherever, to let a queer person know YOU are a safe space for them. A place they can freely express who they are and be authentically themselves. Sometimes just literally saying, 'I'm a safe space for you' is all the reassurance someone needs!

6. SHOW UP FOR THEM

This could be showing up for a queer friend's event to support or even going with them to Pride. These are moments in which your support as an ally is invaluable and won't be forgotten. Furthermore, if you can't physically get somewhere, share their posts, pictures and work on your social channels. Raise and amplify their voices!

CHAPTER FOUR

LOVE YOUR

Queer mental health is uniquely different. We have to regularly deal with so many different emotions and feelings. Existing in the world can be quite overwhelming sometimes, but queer icons are here to remind you that you have got this, you can face it and you can overcome it. Be kind to yourself.

QUEER SELF!

JVN

@jvn

Jonathan Van Ness a.k.a. JVN is a hairdresser, author and star of Netflix's critically acclaimed and gayalicious show *Queer Eye*. JVN identifies as non-binary and was the first non-female to be on the cover of *Cosmopolitan* magazine in 35 years, come through progressivity! Appearing on *Queer Eye* as the hair and beauty expert, JVN shot to fame thanks to his totally adorable personality, sharp wit and words of wisdom for the heroes they make over on the show. *Queer Eye* is known for its emotional moments and Jonathan does not shy away from speaking openly about his own personal journey with his mental health. Completely meme-worthy and viral AF, JVN has cemented himself as a true queer icon in pop culture.

He uses his podcast, *Getting Curious With Jonathan Van Ness*, to promote his activism and to speak on current political and social issues in the United States. I love how knowledgeable he is about so many things. He can give you a homemade solution for dry scalp (apple cider vinegar) but also school you on every presidential candidate in American politics right now (sometimes in the same sentence!).

In November of 2019, he came out as HIV positive, with unanimous support from everyone. Having a figure like Jonathan share their status lets others in the HIV community know they are not alone.

CHAR ELLESSE

@ellessechar

Back in 2017, Char Ellesse set up Girls Will Be Boys, a platform with a mission to challenge gender roles and deconstruct the idea of the gender binary. With this movement, Char shares experiences from women who want to tell their stories about gender identity and self-acceptance alongside the tagline: 'Is it always binary?' Sitting alongside GWBB, is #omgshesbald, a short film and project she created to explore 'modern ideas of femininity through women who have shaved their heads'. It also highlights that women should be able to shave their heads, feel empowered and not have their gender, sexuality or how feminine they are questioned by others.

With a highly engaged following on social media, she uses her captions as a way to engage with her audience and start conversations around racism, queer rights, body positivity and mental health. Talking about how she felt on World Suicide Prevention Day, Char wrote: 'Whether times have been hard or still are, you deserve the help you need to keep on keeping on.'

'LET YOURSELF FEEL AND YOU'LL KNOW WHAT TO DO'

LOTTIE L'AMOUR

@lottielamour

Lottie L'Amour is a body positive, plus-size activist and founder of Love My Chub Club, a platform that 'celebrates diverse fat bodies'. She's also open about her journey with her mental health and actively speaks about times when she is struggling to her audience. It's quite rare for creators on social media to be as transparent as Lottie, but by being so vulnerable to so many, she is actively helping so many other queer people (including me). In one post she wrote: 'Mental health recovery is not linear. There's no magic potion to make you feel better.'

Lottie has won numerous awards for work she has done online and offline around mental health and plus-size representation in the fashion industry. Furthermore, in her job in marketing, working alongside creators, she constantly makes sure she hires queer creators, and not JUST in Pride season. Go Lottie!

'IT'S SO IMPORTANT TO TALK WHEN YOU'RE STRUGGLING, BECAUSE IT'S NOT ALWAYS STRAIGHTFORWARD

ADAM ELI

@adameli

Author Adam Eli has been an unstoppable activist in the queer community in the past few years and is someone I really look up to. He co-founded Voices 4, an NYC-based activist group that's focused on 'queer liberation', and actively uses his social media to talk on a wide range of issues, including everything from dealing with homophobia or anti-Semitism to helping promote and organise rallies and protests during the pandemic. He speaks up for marginalised members of the queer community across the world and uses his voice to amplify theirs.

When Gucci produced their first zine, *Chime For Change*, they turned to Adam to help edit it. Launching it with a huge campaign and full of queer talent, he helped mark a turning point in representation for LGBTQ+ creators in the fashion and print industries. He also frequently touches on body image within the queer community, reminding his audience that all bodies are beautiful. One of my favourite quotes was his tweet: 'this is your permission to unfollow accounts that make you feel bad about your body.'

'I LOVE BEING A QUEER JEW AND NOBODY CAN TAKE THAT AWAY FROM ME'

DEXTER MAYFIELD

@dexrated

Dexter Mayfield is a plus-size model, actor and dancer who pushes for more visibility of plus-size queer people and body positivity within the queer community. He has walked and sashayed down a fashion catwalk for fashion designer Marco Marco, appeared in a J-Lo music video, and amassed a huge audience of fans that love him for his humour, fierce looks and dance moves! I've never seen someone work a designer neon catsuit with matching neon high-heeled boots, but Dexter OWNS it.

He was the first ever queer Black plus-size man to walk a catwalk in LA Fashion Week, which further showed how much more representation is needed in the fashion industry for icons like Dexter. Since that show, his profile has continually grown and he has become a prolific ambassador for men's body positivity. Speaking to *HuffPost* about seeing more plus-size models on billboards, he said, 'I think that so many more young men will be confident in themselves and happy as the person they are if we can do that.'

'I'M NOT GOING TO LET (MY BODY) BE AN EXCUSE FOR SOMEONE TO NOT TREAT ME WITH THE RESPECT, LOVE AND CARE THAT I DESERVE.'

SHIVA RAICHANDANI

@shivaraichandani

A non-binary artist and writer, Shiva Raichandani also writes and speaks about mental health, racism, LGBTQ+ politics and the importance of more gender-diverse representation in the world. As the principal dancer and lead instructor for the London School of Bollywood, she helps lead a dance company that aims to use music and dance to challenge the ways in which gender-diverse people are represented universally and in Bollywood. So far the company has appeared and competed on *Britain's Got Talent* as well as the France and India versions of the series, with Shiva speaking about their routine on the latter: 'With a routine like this in which a non-binary gender fluid "star" takes centre stage instead of the quintessential "hero" and "heroine", we hoped to add to the discourse around gender fluidity and queerness that is too often ignored in the Bollywood industry.'

Shiva created and is also starting production on *Queer Parivaar*, a film set around an interfaith wedding of a queer couple that will cover themes such as the identities of non-binary people, family bonds and, of course, queer LOVE.

JAMIE WINDUST

@jamie_windust

With bold lips, striking stars across their face and a wardrobe I can only dream of pulling off, there is no one out there like Jamie. An author, writer and contributing editor to *GAY TIMES*, Jamie identifies as non-binary and frequently writes and shares their experiences navigating gender dysphoria and transphobia. Jamie openly talks about their mental health and how they deal with it day-to-day and has worked closely with many different charities and organisations.

As a non-binary person, they face a lot of discrimination, and remind their huge audience of followers to be kind to themselves and to keep on fighting. With a huge focus on pushing to keep the Gender Recognition Act, Jamie has actively been working hard to raise awareness around the GRA and how it will benefit gender non-conforming and trans members of the LGBTQ+ community. They wrote: 'Despite everything we portray, many of us are truly devastated and tired, but we WILL fight this.'

'ALWAYS TRY AND REMEMBER THE JOY IN BEING US'

JILLIAN

@jillianmercado

Jillian Mercado is a disabled Latinx actress, activist and model. Modelling for *Diesel, Nordstrom* and *Target* AND appearing in magazines like *Teen Vogue* and *Cosmopolitan*, Jillian is pushing forward for even more representation of wheelchair-bound users and accessibility for them in the media, especially in the fashion industry. She often speaks about how people can be allies to the disabled community and what more they can do to make sure that authentic representation happens. Talking to *Teen Vogue*, she said, 'If you have a position of power to actually be the one to change – or even if you're not – speak up about it.'

Jillian is also the founder of Black Disabled Creatives, a platform to showcase a variety of different Black creatives with disabilities. This is a way for Jillian to create a safe space where she can, she says, help 'bridge the divide for creatives with disabilities'.

'IF YOU FEEL LIKE THE WORLD IS LETTING YOU DOWN, BE THE PERSON TO CHANGE IT'

HAYLEY KIYOKO

@hayleykiyoko

Dubbed by her fans as 'Lesbian Jesus', Hayley Kiyoko is a singer, writer and actress. Her music centres on her own journey with her sexuality and her identity. She released the same-sex romance-themed video, 'Girls Like Girls' in 2015, and aside from it being a certified tune, it has also garnered over 128 million views on YouTube. Like I said, it's a TUNE.

The music industry still has a long way to go in terms of queer representation, and being an openly queer singer like Hayley can take a toll on mental health. Last year she filmed a video for World Suicide Prevention Day and the 'Seize The Awkward' campaign, talking about how she deals with her mental health on a regular basis and the stigma of being a queer singer. She discussed how she had reached a point where she couldn't *not* talk about it – 'When you don't talk about it, you feel more isolated, you feel more alone, and I'm sure many of you go through those feelings . . . we *need* to talk about it.'

CHERYL HOLE

@cherylholequeen

Cheryl Hole is *THE* Essex Diva. One of the first contestants on the first ever series of *RuPaul's Drag Race UK*, Cheryl came, saw, conquered and made a lasting impression on viewers. With her sparkling personality, self-deprecating humour and passion for pop-culture references, she became a firm fan favourite. However, she definitely dealt with some obstacles along the way. Earlier in the series she struggled with the pressure of being on a large televised platform and that was affecting her own state of mind. She came through it though; in a beautiful moment of self-affirmation in her interview, wiping some tears away, she said, 'I'm a f##king star'. You ARE Cheryl!

Being thrust into the spotlight comes with its own fair share of people's negativity and lots of fans reach out to her with their own problems. Being the babe she is, Cheryl always shares helpline numbers, words of advice and important calls to action of how fans can seek support. Just one scroll at her Instagram and you'll find a whole lot of hair, sequins, stunning looks and A LOT of heart.

'WHEN ALL ELSE FAILS, NEVER FORGET... YOU'RE A F##KING STAR!'

RIVER GALLO

@rivergallo

I first came across River Gallo when I was told to watch a short film they had written, directed and acted in called *Ponyboi*. Holy shit, I was not ready for the nineteen-minute emotional rollercoaster that the film took me on, but WOW. Watch it. Repeatedly. *Ponyboi* tells the story of an intersex runaway, played by River, who is looking for love and also trying to navigate their own intersex identity. It's game-changing, heart-breaking and visually stunning. It also FINALLY has representation of an intersex character and actor on film, and truly touches on the topic of what their journey has been and what it is like for so many other intersex people out there.

River is non-binary, queer and a fantastic activist for intersex rights, repeatedly, openly talking about their own experiences, the importance of visibility for characters like Ponyboi, and ending non-consensual surgery on intersex infants and youth. Icons like River need to have their stories told and their characters seen on screen more, so make sure you watch *Ponyboi*, and then share how much you love it on social media. Furthermore, River is currently developing the short into a feature film. YES, RIVER! We'd love to see it!

'BEING A MISFIT CAN BE ONE'S GREATEST GIFT'

SMALL ACTS OF SELF-CARE FOR YOUR MENTAL H E A L T H:

This is a list of things that genuinely work for me. If they don't work for you, do some googling and I'm sure you will find plenty other ideas out there, too. As queer people, we need to look after ourselves and sometimes just doing one of these a day is enough. Give yourself the time you deserve; you are a gift of a human being.

1. MAKE YOUR BED

You will feel like you've achieved something before your day has started. It's a game changer.

2. CREATE

Draw, paint, write a story. You don't even need to be good at it, just do it. Being creative helps you to express how you may be feeling in other ways if you feel you can't articulate it to someone.

3. TAKE A SOCIAL MEDIA BREAK

Having a few days off social media is a great way to re-centre yourself and cut out any overwhelming feelings you've had. Only go back when YOU feel comfortable to.

4. MEET A FRIEND

Seeing a friend and openly talking about what is on your mind can really work. Just make sure it's the right friend, one that will listen, give you a cuddle and eat ice cream with you non-stop all afternoon.

5. MAKE ALLOWANCES FOR YOURSELF

If you're having a good, bad or 'meh' day, that's okay. Don't make yourself feel bad about it.

6. LIGHT A CANDLE

I swear down, a good candle can work and chill you out. Close your eyes for five minutes and do some...

7. BREATHING EXERCISES

Breathe in for 4, hold for 7 and out for 8. This especially works for me when I'm very anxious.

8. RECOGNISE HOW FAR YOU'VE COME

That bad day you had two weeks ago when you were upset and in bed? Two weeks later you've come through that. Remind yourself that whatever you're feeling at that time, you can face it. You can.

9. WERK OUT

I hate working out but a HIIT session or some yoga can really help me refocus on what I'm feeling and what I want to get out of that day.

10. GO FOR A WALK

Fresh air in your lungs is bliss and a walk is a great way to process your thinking.

11. READ A BOOK

Taking a few minutes away from a screen is great for your eyes and hopefully by reading this right now you're feeling that benefit!

12. LISTEN TO CHER

Truthfully, magic always happens when you listen to Cher. Cher is a universal being that transcends time, space and life. Her music will make you feel, dance and shake your hips.

CHAPTER FIVE

PRIDE

It's Pride time! It's the one month of the year when we can celebrate LGBTQ+ rights, push for change and own our QUEER POWER. It's also when loads of brands put together Pride products to sell for one month only, but the less said about that the better ... Pride is a time to remind ourselves of everyone that came before us to fight for the rights we have today. And to be aware of the other areas of the world where LGBTQ+ people are still discriminated against and the further work we need to do!

BILLY PORTER

@theebillyporter

Billy Porter is an actor, singer and frequent server of jaw-droppingly fierce red-carpet looks. If you've watched *Pose*, you'll know him for his beautiful portrayal of Pray Tell, a role which saw him nominated for an Emmy. Billy's profile has continued to grow in the mainstream, along with the gloriously camp fashion moments he gives us, ranging from tuxedo ballgowns at the Oscars, Egyptian god at the Met Gala and *that* fringed-hat moment. He uses these points in his life to redirect attention to the Black Lives Matter movement and LGBTQ+ rights across the world.

Billy performed at the World Pride opening ceremony and London Pride in 2019. At the fully digital NYC Pride in 2020, he did a virtual performance and made sure to reaffirm and remind his audience that whilst there was no physical Pride, there was still a community out there for them: 'Y'all #pride is a bit different this year, however, it's as important to embrace and support our community.'

TAN FRANCE

@tanfrance

Stylist and fashion guru Tan France is one of the first ever openly gay South Asian men to appear on a mainstream TV show, *Queer Eye*. Throughout the show he helps people empower themselves to be their best, most fabulous and authentic self through fashion. Having the responsibility of his representation on such a large scale on a show like this, and gaining over 3 million followers on Instagram, is a big deal! And things just keep getting better for Tan – he has released a book and gone on to front his own fashion show for Netflix, *Next In Fashion*. This is the sort of representation the world needs more of!

Tan also frequently speaks about misconceptions within the LGBTQ+ community and what it's like to be openly gay and of colour. Speaking to *Shortlist*, he addressed the privilege that comes with being white and gay, 'where people are often white and see existing white people in their culture. They see themselves reflected, so they see a sense of acceptance. That's a kind of privilege people don't know they possess.'

'WE MUST ALL BE ALIGNED IN THE MOVEMENT TOWARDS EQUALITY FOR IT TO BE SUCCESSFUL'

LANDON CIDER

@landoncider

Landon Cider is the first drag king to ever compete in a televised drag competition, and, spoiler alert – he won! Appearing in season three of The Boulet Brothers' *Dragula* (check it out), Landon repeatedly delivered show-stopping looks to the show's key themes, Filth, Horror and Glamour. He also spoke about the importance of representation for drag kings and non-binary performers in the drag community. The community has a lot of talented performers who aren't cis men who struggle to get bookings and true visibility, so having Landon on *Dragula* competing alongside non-binary performer Hollow Eve was fantastic to see, and in my personal opinion, so refreshing and important.

Historically, drag kings have been around since the 1900s, but they have been almost erased from queer history; Landon cites Stormé DeLarverie as one of their inspirations. As Landon has pointed out, he believes this is because a lot people have the common misconception that drag kings are less entertaining than drag queens, but this view is rooted in misogyny. So next time you come across a drag performer on social media that isn't a cis man, follow them, support them and share their art.

'I AM A PROUD CIS WOMAN, LESBIAN AND DRAG KING'

CHERYL

@cherylofficial

When pop queen and gay icon Cheryl took to the stage at Manchester Pride in 2019, I got little gay goosebumps. She walked out wearing a black sequinned jumpsuit with rainbow-coloured fastenings and a huge rainbow striped cloak. As she did, a monologue voiced by her played to the crowd reaffirming her message of equal rights for the LGBTQ+ community: 'Together, tonight we are celebrating the right to love and be loved by whomever we choose in our lifetime and I believe we should fight for this love.' Turning her cloak to the crowd, it was pulled out to reveal handwritten typography saying 'FIGHT FOR THIS LOVE' (fun fact: typography by me) and the crowd went wild.

This was a great moment of allyship from Cheryl for the Pride attendees and also something that united so many that night. For me, there is a special power that is felt when one of your idols acknowledges your existence and your rights. And doing it all with an inclusive Pride flag colourway on the outfit, too? Perfection.

'IT'S IMPORTANT FOR SOMEONE LIKE ME, IN A POSITION WHERE PEOPLE LISTEN TO WHAT I'VE GOT TO SAY, TO SPREAD THAT MESSAGE OF LOVE'

OUTFIT DESIGNED by JACK IRVING STUDIO!

STYLED by ANNA Hughes-CHAMBERLAIN

FIGHT FOR THIS LOVE

AARON PHILIP

@aaron___philip

Signing with Elite Model Management at eighteen years old, Aaron Philip became the first Black transgender wheelchair user to do so. Since then she's been featured in numerous fashion publications, shows AND even been interviewed by Naomi Campbell for *Paper* magazine. She is heavily focused on getting better visibility for disabled people and is on a mission to make sure this happens, so that disabled people everywhere know they're not alone and they're *seen*.

Aaron uses her social media to educate and involve her audience about the LGBTQ+ community. She reposts GoFundMe pages for those struggling financially, resource posts, and continually speaks about how people can be an ally. During the beginning of Pride week, she wrote: 'Be more than an ally, learn to love, protect and understand Black trans people.'

'LOVE BLACK TRANS PEOPLE AS MUCH AS YOU LOVE YOURSELF AND FIGHT FOR US THAT WAY'

SCHUYLER BAILAR

@pinkmantaray

In 2015, Schuyler Bailar became the first openly transgender athlete to swim in NCAA Division I history. At the time this was, and still is, a huge step forward for how trans athletes are viewed in sport. Originally, Schuyler swam for Harvard on the women's team but took a break for his mental health and to reassess. Eventually, his female coach on the women's team spoke to the coach of the men's team, as she wanted what was best for him, especially as he was transitioning at the time. The men's team took Schuyler on.

Since then Schuyler has gone on to be heavily involved in activism for the trans and LGBTQ+ community. He helped with the USA Swimming cultural inclusion guides for LGBTQ+ and Asian American Athletes. On Instagram, he is known for posing alongside a whiteboard on which he writes key messages around a number of current social and political issues. Each post differs, with subjects ranging from mental health to racism to trans rights. Posting about Pride season during the pandemic and Black Lives Matter protests, he reminded his audience, 'The first Pride was a police riot'.

SHEA COULEÉ

@sheacoulee

If you've watched *RuPaul's Drag Race*, Shea Couleé will be a familiar name. A drag queen, musician and activist, Shea has said it's important to her to use her career and platform to inspire people, especially Black women and drag performers: 'My Drag in its purest form is a love letter to Black women.' She serves looks that always have a narrative and message linked to them for her audience to pick up on and learn from.

A firm fan favourite with a loyal following, Shea also utilises her community to engage in her activism work and speak up against racism. The same month as Pride 2020, she was spotted at the Drag March for Change in support of Black Lives Matter. Someone recorded a video of her, out of drag, taking to the stage to speak to a crowd of protesters: 'We need to make space. If y'all want to see it for us, pull up and open your purse. My name is Shea Couleé and I didn't come to play; I came to dismantle white supremacy.'

'IT IS MY DUTY AS A BLACK PERSON, AND AS A BLACK PERSON WITH A PLATFORM, TO SPEAK OUT ABOUT THIS'

TRAVIS ALABANZA

@travisalabanza

A lot of people in this book are multi-talented – and Travis Alabanza is no exception! Identifying as trans-feminine and gender non-conforming, Travis is a writer, actor, performer and theatre maker. Growing up as Black and queer in Bristol, they would use art to help them navigate and deal with the ignorance they were facing at the time. Cut to 2020, and they are one of the most prolific creatives on the queer scene, performing solo plays, speaking at (over 40) universities, and consistently using their online platform to speak up for change for the trans and gender non-conforming communities.

During Pride season, trans and non-binary people don't always get the chance to take up the space their cis white queer counterparts do. Speaking to *GAY TIMES*, Travis mentioned how the gay community still has work to do to help the trans community, especially around Pride season: '. . . care about how we're getting home from the party. I think for me that is the focal point: to see us outside of just being fierce and to see us also as just people.'

YOUNG BLACK LGBTQ+ KIDS DESERVE
ROLE MODELS, POSSIBILITIES,
AND THE ABILITY TO REFLECT
AND CONNECT WITH THEIR
HISTORY

'INTERSECTIONALITY IS REAL, FINDING SOMEWHERE TO BELONG IS BEAUTIFUL, & I LOVE BEING A GAY MAN'

@mnek

MNEK is a Grammy-nominated chart-topping singer and songwriter. You most likely have heard one of his hits, whether it's sung by him or written by him. He has worked with a long list of huge musical talents including Beyoncé, Little Mix, Dua Lipa, Christina Aguilera and Madonna, to name just a FEW (the list is endless). In 2018, he released his first solo album entitled *Language* and headlined UK Black Pride that same year. I can safely say that album is full of certified bops, including 'Tongue', the lead single, the video for which featured MNEK vogueing in a hot pink matching shirt and trousers combo that, to be honest, is an iconic moment.

Aside from headlining at various queer events, he is a huge advocate for the queer community and also pushes for more representation in the music industry for Black and PoC queer people. Teaming up with Pride In Music in 2019, MNEK hosted a writing camp for LGBTQ+ songwriters for them to write, create and produce with a number of other queer performers, to help them gain further opportunities in music.

AS LONG AS MY PEOPLE DON'T HAVE THEIR RIGHTS ALL ACROSS AMERICA, THERE'S NO REASON FOR CELEBRATION

Marsha P. Johnson's legacy will never be forgotten. An African-American transgender activist and trailblazer, she was a prominent figure in the origins of Pride and did a lot of work for the queer rights movement in the 1960s and 70s. She said the 'P' stood for 'Pay it no mind', a phrase she would use when someone had something transphobic to say about her appearance. A sex worker and drag performer, Marsha was an essential part of the New York City gay scene in Greenwich Village and also during the Stonewall riots and the protests that followed. She was passionate about social justice and getting equal rights for everyone, especially the trans and Black trans community. She was known for her infectious smile, warm personality and visual aesthetic of bright wigs, flowers and limitless kindness and generosity.

During the Stonewall riots, Marsha P. Johnson and a number of other queer people resisted arrest. This led to a series of protests and riots and a month later, the first organised queer rights march took place in New York City. In 1992, Marsha went missing and her body was found six days later. To this day the Black trans community are still extremely vulnerable. Over 44 trans or gender non-conforming people were killed in the US in 2020, the majority of which were Black and Latinx trans women.

MARSHA
P. JOHNSON

SYLVIA RIVERA

'WE HAVE TO BE VISIBLE. WE SHOULD NOT BE ASHAMED OF WHO WE ARE'

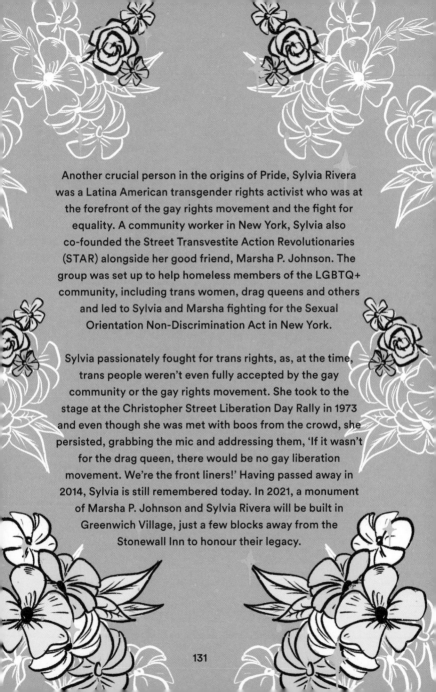

Another crucial person in the origins of Pride, Sylvia Rivera was a Latina American transgender rights activist who was at the forefront of the gay rights movement and the fight for equality. A community worker in New York, Sylvia also co-founded the Street Transvestite Action Revolutionaries (STAR) alongside her good friend, Marsha P. Johnson. The group was set up to help homeless members of the LGBTQ+ community, including trans women, drag queens and others and led to Sylvia and Marsha fighting for the Sexual Orientation Non-Discrimination Act in New York.

Sylvia passionately fought for trans rights, as, at the time, trans people weren't even fully accepted by the gay community or the gay rights movement. She took to the stage at the Christopher Street Liberation Day Rally in 1973 and even though she was met with boos from the crowd, she persisted, grabbing the mic and addressing them, 'If it wasn't for the drag queen, there would be no gay liberation movement. We're the front liners!' Having passed away in 2014, Sylvia is still remembered today. In 2021, a monument of Marsha P. Johnson and Sylvia Rivera will be built in Greenwich Village, just a few blocks away from the Stonewall Inn to honour their legacy.

STORMÉ
DE LARVERIE

Stormé DeLarverie was an entertainer, activist and a drag king who often performed as part of the Jewel Box Revue, which in 1955 was North America's first racially integrated drag cabaret, which toured around the country. At that time there weren't many drag kings around, never mind performing, and, even over 50 years later, they are still underrepresented (as Landon Cider pointed out earlier). Then not in her drag persona, Stormé was known off-stage for her gender non-conforming appearance, embracing her androgyny and often styling herself in men's suits and hats. This led to her being photographed by the influential and iconic Diane Arbus.

Working as a bouncer and volunteer street worker, Stormé was seen as a fierce protector of the lesbian community in New York City. During the Stonewall uprising, many butch lesbians were there that night and many believe she was the person who encouraged the crowd to fight back against the police, with eyewitnesses saying a woman fitting her appearance resisted arrest numerous times, was handcuffed and hit over the head by a policeman with a baton. She turned to the crowd watching and allegedly said, 'Why don't you guys do something?' As she was loaded into the back of a police vehicle, the crowd began to stir and rise up against what was happening. For the 50th anniversary of the Stonewall riots in 2019, the Stonewall National Monument was unveiled which honoured 50 American prominent figures as part of the National LGBTQ Wall Of Honor (this sits within the SNM). Stormé was one of them.

'**NO** TO RACISM.
TO HOMOPHOBIA
TO BIPHOBIA.
TO TRANSPHOBIA
TO ISLAMOPHOBIA.
PUT YOUR FISTS UP
IN SOLIDARITY!'

@ladyphyll

There are not enough words to describe my love and adoration for Phyll Opoku-Gyimah, a.k.a. Lady Phyll. She is the co-founder, trustee and executive director of UK Black Pride – the UK's biggest LGBTQ+ event and safe space for queer Black people and queer people of colour.

I went to my first UK Black Pride only a few years ago. It was THE most important Pride event I have been to. It promoted inclusivity, equality and anti-racism. Lady Phyll takes to the stage and her words galvanise and stir a crowd, reminding a whole intersectional part of our queer community how important they are and how their voices need to be raised.

In 2016, Phyll turned down the opportunity to receive the MBE in the New Year Honours List. She told *DIVA* magazine, 'As a trade unionist, a working-class girl and an out Black African lesbian, I want to stand to my principles and values.' And that she DID.

Lady Phyll has continued to speak up and encourages others to do so. At the 2019 World Pride celebrations in New York City, she was invited on to the main stage where she took to the mic, fist held high in the air, to say, 'No to racism. No to homophobia. No to biphobia. No to transphobia. No to islamophobia. Put your fists up in solidarity!'

Icon. Queen. Trailblazer. Thank you, Lady Phyll, for everything you do.

WAYS TO CELEBRATE PRIDE SEASON ALL YEAR ROUND:

Pride is ALL THE TIME, baby. Here are some ways to find queerness in everyday life and celebrate yourself and your community with loved ones.

1 – READ, LISTEN AND WATCH

Every year there is new LGBTQ+ content released. Netflix even has its own LGBTQ+ section now. This means you can stream queer shows, listen to queer music and read queer books. Immerse yourself in the culture and community. You'll be educated, inspired and proud.

2 – SUPPORT QUEER FUNDS AND CHARITIES

There are numerous queer funds and charities that need your support. Instead of spending a tenner on a rainbow fan, consider donating that money to a charity. If you can't financially support, share the charity's page on your socials and let your friends know. I think it's important to give back to the community, especially supporting charities or funds centred around Black or PoC queer people. As a white cis queer man, I'm aware of my privilege and what I can do to help those marginalised in our community.

3 – GO TO LGBTQ+ STUFF

You can attend a number of events, art shows, plays, museum exhibitions and more throughout the year that have LGBTQ+ themes. These are great ways to celebrate Pride and also support the talent involved!

4 – REACH OUT

There are times where we will need a friend or a family member. Do not hesitate to reach out to somebody who can listen and love you. Being queer is an experience that is unique to each of us and at times we can be triggered and need to talk. There is also nothing wrong with using a helpline with a qualified volunteer on the other end. Don't be alone in your feelings.

5 – THROW AN EVENT

There's nothing stopping you having family, chosen family and friends over for a night of proud anthems. A glitter curtain will change your life FOR EVER. Get some cocktails going, put some tunes on, steal Aunty Carol's disco leggings from the 80s and have your very own queer safe space party!

6 – DRESS TO IMPRESS

I love to serve a lewk on the way to the bus stop, and there's nothing stopping you either! Not all queer people are queer 'presenting'; however, if you want to dress that way, do it. You can celebrate your rainbowtasticness and identity through experimenting with fashion, styling and make-up. And don't forget to own the street like a catwalk when you do. WERK!

7 – SHARE ON YOUR SOCIAL

Use your social media to share LGBTQ+-related content to help your followers understand we're still fighting for LGBTQ+ rights across the world.

8 – BUY A GLITTER CURTAIN

If you didn't get the hint before, you really need to, hun. They will take your space from cute kitchen to DISCO ELEGANZA.

OUTRO

There isn't one way to be 'queer'. Personally, I found this out at an early age when I genuinely thought all gay men were meant to act like Jack in *Will & Grace*. Whilst some do, I could NOT pull off that look. Don't forget what makes up the brilliant DNA of YOU. Queer people come in all shapes, sizes, personalities and fabulousness, and however you feel you *should* be, don't – just BE. For the record, this book and myself totally accept you and I'm sending you a big invisible hug right now. You got this. And whilst you've read this book on queer icons and their stories, take a minute to think of your story, your life and what you've navigated to be here – you're an icon yourself and you have that queer power inside of you. Always.

THANK YOU!

This book is dedicated to my friends Anick Soni, Blair Imani, Tess Holliday, Freida Slaves, Julian Gavino, Alexander Leon, Arun Blair-Mangat, Kenny Ethan Jones, Juno Dawson, Radam Ridwan, Charlie Craggs, Crystal Rasmussen, Sabah Choudrey, Jade Thirlwall, TeTe Bang, Tanya Compass, Cheddar Gorgeous, Jessie Ware, Char Ellesse, Lottie L'Amour, Adam Eli, Shiva Raichandani, Jamie Windust, Cheryl Hole, River Gallo, Cheryl, Travis Alabanza, MNEK, Lady Phyll ... and my mum, Madeleine.

I also want to take a minute to thank all the icons who were involved in this book and have supported it. It's truly been a dream of mine to create a book that amplifies voices in the LGBTQ+ community that need to be heard more, so THANK YOU for being part of this journey! Rainbows and cuddles to all of you. A big Thank You to the whole team at HarperCollins for all the support. This book was created, drawn and written whilst my mum was suffering a heart attack AND during a pandemic. The support was everything and it really helped me focus during a really stressful time. Omara, you have been a total legend and have really worked with me to create such a queertastic book, thank you! Lydia, thank you so much for all the work you did in setting this project up and putting up with my ramblings on Zoom calls. Thank you to the whole design team at HarperCollins who have laid out the pages, arranged illustrations and done so much work on it. It's a paper eleganza, huns! Thank you. Big Thank You to Lauren Gardner, aka The LG, for continually being a great agent, someone who has my best interests at heart, listens and is still my own little personal rainbow. I'm very lucky to have an LG. Lastly, a big thanks to all my family and friends who have supported me throughout this process and been total babes. I love you all! And finally, thank YOU to whoever is reading this. Thank you for supporting this book, these voices and these messages. Take them with you into the world and share the love.

WAYS TO SUPPORT

On these pages are just *some* of the different organisations and funds you can support or contact if you need support . . .

ALBERT KENNEDY TRUST – an LGBTQ+ youth homelessness charity working with young people aged 16–25 who are struggling with their housing situation or living in a hostile, violent or abusive environment. @aktcharity

BLACK TRANS FEMMES IN THE ARTS – a collective of Black trans femmes dedicated to creating space in the arts and beyond. @btfacollective

COLOURS YOUTH NETWORK – supports young people of colour to explore and celebrate who they are through events, workshops and more. @coloursyouthuk

EXIST LOUDLY FUND – an organisation for queer Black youth to find a community, a chosen family and explore their identity through digital and online workshops. @existloudly

GENDERED INTELLIGENCE – a trans-led charity working across the UK to increase understandings of gender diversity. @genderedintelligence

IMAAN LGBTQI MUSLIM SUPPORT – the leading LGBTQ+ Muslim organisation. @imaanlgbtqi

LGBT FOUNDATION – a national charity delivering services, advice and support for LGBT people in England. @lgbtfdn

MERMAIDS GENDER – supports gender-diverse kids, young people and their families. @mermaidsgender

OPENING DOORS LONDON – a charity providing services and support for LGBTQ+ people over 50. @openingdoorslondon

STONEWALL UK – a lesbian, gay, bisexual and transgender rights charity that campaigns for LGBTQ+ equality. @stonewalluk

UK BLACK PRIDE – Europe's largest celebration for African, Asian, Middle Eastern, Latin American and Caribbean-heritage LGBTQ people. @ukblackpride

HELPLINES

If you need to reach out, and just have a talk, you can always call these numbers, text or do live chat with these links.

ALBERT KENNEDY TRUST Live chat at www.akt.org.uk

CHILDLINE 0800 1111

GENDERED INTELLIGENCE 0330 3559 678

LGBT FOUNDATION 0345 3 30 30 30

MERMAIDS 0808 801 0400

SAMARITANS 116 123

SHOUT 85258

Text PRIDE to 85258 to talk to a SHOUT volunteer www.giveusashout.org/get-help/

SWITCHBOARD LGBT+ HELPLINE 0300 330 0630

RESOURCES

WATCH IT!

THE INTERSEX DIARIES
(documentary, BBC Radio 1 Stories)
POSE (drama series, FX)
PARIS IS BURNING
(documentary film, 1990)
SEX EDUCATION
(comedy-drama series, Netflix)
QUEER EYE (reality show, Netflix)
RUPAUL'S DRAG RACE (reality
show, Logo TV/VH1)
THE BOULET BROTHERS'
DRAGULA (reality show,
Netflix/Amazon Prime)
PRIDE (feature film, 2014)
DISCLOSURE
(documentary, Netflix)
LEGENDARY (reality show, HBO)
PAY IT NO MIND – THE LIFE
AND TIMES OF MARSHA P.
JOHNSON (documentary, 2012)
A FANTASTIC WOMAN
(feature film, 2017)
PONYBOI (feature film, 2019)
SPECIAL (comedy series, Netflix)

STREAM IT!

LANGUAGE by MNEK (album)
SAWAYAMA by Rina
Sawayama (album)
'LOVE YOURSELF'
by Billy Porter (song)
PALO SANTO
by Years & Years (album)
CONFETTI by Little Mix (album)
'FIGHT FOR THIS LOVE'
by Cheryl (song)
CLARITY by Kim Petras (album)
CHROMATICA by
Lady Gaga (album)
WHAT'S YOUR PLEASURE?
by Jessie Ware (album)
111 by Pabllo Vittar (album)

READ IT!

MAKING OUR WAY HOME: THE GREAT MIGRATION AND THE BLACK AMERICAN DREAM By Blair Imani (Ten Speed Press, 2020)

THE GENDER GAMES: THE PROBLEM WITH MEN AND WOMEN, FROM SOMEONE WHO HAS BEEN BOTH By Juno Dawson (Two Roads, 2017)

THE NEW QUEER CONSCIENCE By Adam Eli (Penguin Workshop, 2020)

BEYOND THE GENDER BINARY By Alok Vaid-Menon (Penguin Workshop, 2020)

THE BLACK FLAMINGO By Dean Atta (Hodder, 2019)

NATURALLY TAN: A MEMOIR By Tan France (Virgin Books, 2019)

THE TRANSSEXUAL FROM TOBAGO By Dominique Jackson (CreateSpace, 2014)

LOCKDOWN LOOKBOOK By Radam Ridwan (2020)

TO MY TRANS SISTERS Edited by Charlie Craggs (Jessica Kingsley, 2017)

OVER THE TOP: MY STORY By Jonathan van Ness (Simon & Schuster, 2019)

IN THEIR SHOES: NAVIGATING NON-BINARY LIFE By Jamie Windust (Jessica Kingsley, 2020)

FREE TO BE ME: AN LGBTQ+ JOURNAL OF LOVE, PRIDE & FINDING YOUR INNER RAINBOW By Dom&Ink (Penguin, 2019)

LISTEN TO IT!

QMMUNITY (podcast)
ANTHEMS (podcast)
A GAY AND A NONGAY (podcast)

SOURCES

p11 *The Intersex Diaries,* BBC Radio 1 Stories, 2018; p14 'I'm Coming Out', NikkieTutorials, YouTube, 2020; p19 *Nylon,* 2019; p21 'Partly why Freida is still Freida is so … You see a Black drag queen, just living her best life': 'A Celebration of London's Diverse, Queer Drag Culture' by Jess Kohl; p27 *NME,* March 2020; p28 – 'It allows me to embrace my otherness; it celebrates that': *Attitude,* January 2020; p31 *Vulture,* April 2019; p38 TomboyX, 2018; p46 'The big problem for non-binary people like me isn't just being seen – it's being seen as human': *PinkNews,* July 2020; p49 *ELLE* magazine, May 2019; p61 *GAY TIMES* Amplify, July 2020; p62 Dwyane Wade on *The Ellen Show,* February 2020; p65 *Attitude,* May 2020; p66 *Attitude,* April 2019; p68 Stonewall rally, June 2019; p70 *Vogue,* 27 June 2020; p72 *GAY TIMES,* 2019; p75 *Dazed Digital,* November 2019; p77 *GAY TIMES,* 2019; p78 *GAY TIMES,* June 2020; p85 *New York Times,* October 2019; p93 Attitude, July 2020; p98 *GAY TIMES,* 2019; p101 *Billboard,* March 2018; p104 *Subvrt,* June 2020; p111 *Evening Standard,* July 2019; p112 *Image,* 10 June 2020; p115 *GAY TIMES,* 2019; p116 *GAY TIMES,* August 2019; p120 *The Grace Gazette,* October 2019; p123 *Esquire,* June 2020; p124 *Metro,* October 2019.